How to Write

Better Business Letters

A practical, step-by-step discussion of the principles involved and the procedure to be followed in the preparation and dictation of successful letters.

by Earle A. Buckley

Direct Mail Consultant and Letter Specialist, Founder and Former Owner of The Buckley Organization, an Advertising Agency specializing in Mail Selling and Correspondence Improvement.

McGRAW-HILL BOOK COMPANY, INC.

New York • Toronto • London

HOW TO WRITE BETTER BUSINESS LETTERS

First McGraw-Hill Paperback Edition, 1971

07-008779-2

Preface

Somewhere or other, a ten-year-old boy picked up the idea that the first sentence in a letter should be newsy or interesting enough to make the reader want to read on. At camp for the first full summer away from home, he unconsciously utilized this cardinal principle of good letter writing, but forgot that there is more to a letter than just a first sentence. Here is his message in full—

Dear Mother:
    The most exciting thing has just happened.
                              Your loving son,
                                 Tony

Exciting perhaps, but definitely unsatisfying at the receiving end. And so are thousands and thousands of letters that are put into the mail every day in the week.

How satisfying are the letters *you* write? How effective? How resultful?

No matter how good they are or how poor, you can make them *better* if (1) you have the *right attitude* and (2) you have the *right knowledge* of fundamental principles. Let me explain.

When you have any kind of a business letter to write, whether sales, inquiry, claim, adjustment, collection, credit, or application, you can look on it as a *chore* or as an *opportunity*.

If you look on it as just a necessary routine, something that must be done but in which there is little pleasure or satisfaction, then the result will be nowhere near your best efforts. Like many other activities, you get out of letter writing in proportion to what you put into it.

On the other hand, if you look on it as an *opportunity* to help someone better understand you, your company, your product, or some unusual situation; an opportunity to change an opinion, make a friend, create a sale, sell an idea, or accomplish some other worth-while objective, then you start the letter in an entirely different frame of mind.

You then write with the express purpose of *accomplishing something,* not just performing a necessary but uninteresting business function. That is what I mean by having the *right attitude.* And if you don't have it now, you can easily acquire it.

That is also true of *knowledge,* the technical know-how needed in every endeavor.

The purpose of this book is to provide that basic knowledge so necessary to a well-constructed letter. If you want to write better letters—friendlier, more convincing, more resultful— I believe the careful reading of this book will help you. It wasn't prepared for the professional letter writer, but rather for the many thousands of men and women who perhaps write good letters now but who could write *outstanding* letters with a little of the right kind of study and application.

Joseph Conrad, Polish-born English novelist, once wrote: "My task, which I am trying to achieve, is by the power of the written word, to make you *hear,* to make you *feel*—it is, before all, to make you *see.*"

That is *your* task, too, whenever you write a letter—to make your reader *see* your product or proposition so vividly that he will be receptive to any reasonable *action* you propose.

The reading of this book will, I hope, make that task

easier. If it does nothing else, it will certainly make you letter-conscious, and that in itself is worth while.

Letter writing today is a profession, an art. Don't take it too much for granted. Don't just dash off a so-called *sales* letter and send it out, hoping it will do an effective job—or hurriedly and thoughtlessly dictate a routine business letter, satisfied if it just answers another.

There's *power* in a good letter, and not to take advantage of it is an economic waste. Remember that by their very customs and traditions people are vitally interested in letters. Of all the different kinds of mail received, letters are invariably opened *first,* and that's true whether the address on the envelope is handwritten or typewritten.

So your letter has a decided advantage to begin with. It is almost certain to be opened and at least scanned. Whether it it *read, assimilated, and acted upon* depends to a large extent on the way you have put your thoughts together, on the *construction* of your message.

If I have done a good job in "How to Write Better Business Letters," you should be able to apply immediately the information this book contains to your own individual problems.

I hope sincerely that you can and that in a short while every one of the letters you turn out will be a *sales letter* in every sense of the term, regardless of its primary purpose.

EARLE A. BUCKLEY

Contents

CHAPTER ONE *Analysis*

Analyzing the Product, Service, or Idea

The Product

Before we do anything else—let's see what we have to sell.

Let's haul it out into plain view, take it apart, and find out something about it. If it's a product, let's study it awhile to determine the features that will enable us to discuss it intelligently. What interests us most, I think, is the excuse it has for existence. What is it? What does it look like? What does it do? How is it used? Why is it better?

Let's be curious about it and ask all the questions we can think of, even at the risk of getting ourselves classed as infernal nuisances. The thing to remember is that the more we know about it, the more easily, more interestingly, and more convincingly we can talk about it in a letter.

We should be able to assume that the product itself will bear close inspection; that it is *right* from a mechanical, chemical, or engineering standpoint; that it actually *will* do the work claimed for it; that its price is economically correct; that it is packaged, labeled, and merchandised in a way calculated to produce the most satisfactory results. It is not the purpose of this book to delve into the intricate problems of real product analysis, but I do want to emphasize the necessity for knowing intimately the full story concerning whatever it is you intend to write about.

The Service

Much the same applies if the letter is about an intangible, a service of some kind. Take *it* apart just as you would a product. See what there is about it that would make *you* want to subscribe to it or want it if you were on the other side of the fence! What does it accomplish that similar services don't or can't? In analyzing it, try very hard to be unbiased. Look at it as far as possible from the other fellow's viewpoint. After all, a service isn't worth a hoot unless it *brings* something, *gives* something, or *does* something worth while for the chap who buys it. Elementary? Of course it is, but a point very often forgotten in the routine carrying on of a business.

The Idea

It may not be a product or service that you have to sell. It may be an *idea*. You may want to sell someone on the idea of lending you $50, or giving you a job, or sending you some money that is owed you, or being a pleased customer again after he's told you in no uncertain terms what an unfair and unreasonable "louse" you really are.

Whatever the idea, you have something definite to sell that you can analyze and take apart just like a product or service. This "taking apart" is a tremendously important requirement in successful letter writing. You can't write a good letter without it, any more than you can drive an automobile without looking where you're going.

Analyzing the Prospect or Customer

We are still "taking apart," but this time it's the person to whom the letter is going. Before writing, it is quite necessary that we know something about the fellow (male or female) at the "other end of the wire."

You wouldn't write to a man in the same way you'd write to a woman, in most cases at least. You certainly wouldn't talk the same "language" to a business executive as to a jobber's salesman. People in different occupations or different stations in life or even different parts of the country often require entirely different kinds of approach.

"To what kind of people am I writing?" is therefore an important question, and a careful analysis in this direction will invariably pay big dividends. When you're just writing to one person—and it's an important letter—it is always good policy, if you can do it, to learn something about him before you start to draft the letter. It may be that you'll want to open up with some reference to a hobby of his, or mention some incident with which you know he is familiar, or avoid some idiosyncrasy.

I know one man, for instance, who is literally a fanatic on the subject of English construction. He likes to take words apart and study them for weeks at a time, trying to find their true meanings. Using colloquialisms or words with a double meaning in writing to that man is like waving a red flag in front of a bull.

If it is a sales letter to a group and you can classify your prospects in any way, as farmers, dealers, professional men, engineers, architects, etc., it is usually quite easy to learn something about them as a group beforehand.

When you have exhausted the possibilities in this direction, the next step is an analysis of the prospect's (or customer's) probable mental attitude. Will he welcome what you are going to say? Will he be glad to hear from you and willing to read everything you send him—or indifferent to any proposition you might make? Will he be open-minded or prejudiced? In order to get action, will you have to change completely some accepted opinion or will his views on the general subject be pretty much in accord with yours? The successful letter writer, if he can't find out for sure, will *sense* the answers to these questions—and be right in a large percentage of cases. The very fact that you've *thought* about them will clear the atmosphere and enable you to write a better letter.

Analyzing the Proposition

There's still some more analyzing to be done before you start to write, so don't be impatient.

You've taken apart the product, service, or idea, whatever it is you have to sell. And you've thought hard about the person to whom your letter is going. Now, to complete the job, let's dissect the *proposition*.

Let's say we have a twelve-year-old "Chevvy." That's the product. An analysis would bring out the few remaining good features of the car and give us our line-up of sales arguments. Understand, the car is a good "buy" at a certain price. It still looks pretty good, and it still runs. But if we attempt in the letter to sell it for $1,000 when the published book value is only a few hundred, then we haven't got a good proposition.

If you're a manufacturer and your price is such that jobbers and dealers can't sell as many of your products or make as much on them as they can with a competitive line, then *you* haven't a good proposition.

Analyze your proposition, whatever it is, before you attempt to exploit it in a letter. Decide whether or not you, in the other fellow's place, would consider it a good "deal." If not, don't write the letter at all. Work on the proposition, and make it attractive enough to justify writing a letter about.

If it *is* a good deal, go to it and sell it for all you're worth.

CHAPTER TWO *The Formula for Sales Letters*

A letter formula is as necessary to sales-letter writing as a recipe is to cake baking. It is something to be learned by heart and followed systematically until it becomes automatic—much the same as the motions used in driving an automobile. The experienced driver isn't conscious of pushing out his left foot every time he changes gears. Neither is the seasoned letter writer conscious of adhering to a letter formula. If his training has been along right lines, he just does it automatically. The formula for writing a sales letter is *interest, desire, conviction,* and *action.* And you can't write a good sales letter without these elements. You must arouse interest, or the reader won't even finish the letter. You must create a desire for whatever you're selling, or obviously you can't hope ultimately to consummate a sale. You must make your reasons for buying convincing, or the prospect won't feel that it is to his advantage to buy. And you must lead him into some kind of action, otherwise his enthusiasm will cool off before you have a chance to "cash in."

This following of a formula in writing sales letters is fundamental. Elementary as it may sound, you can't dispense with it, any more than you can in personal selling.

When you call on a man to interest him in some laborsaving device, for instance, you don't open up by asking him to buy. You tell him something about it that will immediately arouse his interest or curiosity. Then you tell him something about it that will create a desire for it, such as the amount of money he can save every year through its use. Then you bring forth proof to show him that your product will do what you claim for it. And finally you attempt to close the sale.

The procedure is precisely the same in writing an advertisement. Authorities agree that an ad, to be effective, must be seen, read, believed, and acted upon. The first requirement, that it be "seen," obviously doesn't apply to letters, but the other three are equally essential in writing a sales letter. The ad won't be read, believed, and acted upon unless it *does* arouse interest, create desire, inspire conviction, and take the steps necessary to bring about a favorable decision. Students of letter writing should, therefore, commit this formula to memory and use it to check and double check every sales letter they write. There isn't a safer measuring stick available to them.

To impress it further on your mind, let's put the formula in chart form and look at it step by step.

Suppose we start with a straight line and on it indicate a point representing the state of mind of a prospect when first approached—cold, uninterested, but open-minded.

We have a sales job to do on that prospect. So let's draw another line, up higher, representing the frame of mind that the prospect must be in before he will *accept* our proposition and do what we want him to do. (See illustration at top of page 7.)

The first thing to do in writing a sales letter of any kind is to get the reader *interested,* to pave the way for the proposition you are going to spring on him later. When you have accomplished that, you have the first ingredient necessary in

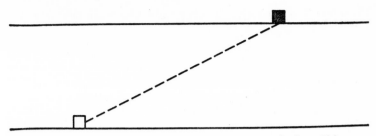

all sales letters—INTEREST. I don't mean curiosity. You can start a sales letter with a statement that might arouse some curiosity as to what it is all about but wouldn't be a good opening if it didn't also arouse INTEREST.

Something of INTEREST to the prospect is, therefore, our first consideration. All right, let's say we have it and have advanced a step in the selling process.

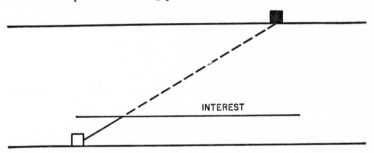

We received a sales letter the other day which started off like this—

The sign says—"Wet Paint." What do you do—touch it?

The cover on a pad of matches reads "Close Cover Before Striking." Do you live dangerously and ignore this suggestion?

On a one-way street there's always the urge to head in, so you blunt the arrow.

"Don't Touch the Flowers" and you walk off with a hand full of pollen.

These and many more instances point up the fact that it's just human nature to react in reverse. Any kid will tell you "don't" is the most inviting inducement to "do."

The next paragraph attempted the transition to the main subject of the letter, but it was too late—*we had already lost interest!* Into the wastebasket it went.

The second job is to create DESIRE, which you do by talking benefits to the reader. That may sound textbookish, but it's practical nevertheless. I have been writing sales letters professionally for many years and still use this same formula.

You create DESIRE by drawing a mental picture of the advantages the reader will enjoy if he buys the service or product or accepts the proposition. DESIRE, then, is the second ingredient in the formula for writing sales letters. Notice how we are getting closer to that state of mind necessary for complete acceptance.

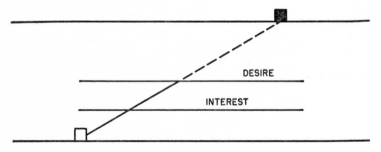

We want to go up another notch now, which we do by establishing CONVICTION in the mind of the reader and acceptance of the fact that we can live up to the "pretty picture" we've drawn in the first and second paragraphs—in other words, satisfactory *proof* that we are going to be able to deliver the advantages we talked about.

If I were to say to you "How would you like a 50 per cent increase in salary?" I'm sure I would have your INTEREST. Then if I pictured for you the benefits of such an increase, what you could do with the extra money you'd have—in short, the advantages that would be yours from this theoretical increase in salary—I would be creating DESIRE. But what good is it if I establish INTEREST and create DESIRE, if there is no CONVICTION in your minds that I will be able to "deliver the goods"? So CONVICTION, or BELIEVABILITY, is the third ingredient in the sales-letter formula—*and a most important one it is.*

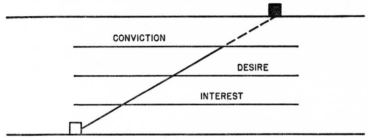

Now if we have gone that far, wouldn't it be foolish not to take the next step and urge some kind of ACTION? We have got to the point where we want the reader to *do something about it.* That means asking for and if possible giving a good reason for taking some kind of *action.*

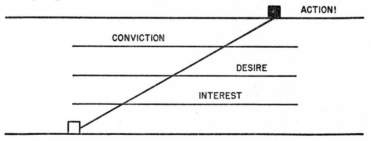

The same theory about selling applies no matter what you have to sell, even if it's only an idea.

CHAPTER THREE *Writing the Opening*

Item one in the sales-letter formula, as you of course know because by now you have carefully memorized it, is *interest*.

Creating interest in the opening paragraph of a letter is as vital as getting off to a good start in a public speech. The opening of a letter is really *more* important than the start of a speech because the chap reading the letter can, and frequently does, throw the letter away if his interest isn't aroused, whereas those listening to a speaker are usually "stuck" until the end, whether he's good, bad, or indifferent. Hence, in beginning a letter, ask yourself, "What can I lead off with, that will make the recipient want to hear more?"

* * *

Right here, let's differentiate between attention and interest. Attracting attention and arousing interest are two entirely different things. Some opening paragraphs attract attention, but they don't arouse interest. On the other hand, if you scare up some interest, you needn't worry about attention. You'll have it. To cite an exaggerated case, starting a letter with "How's your Aunt Minnie?" will no doubt attract attention and lead the reader on, through curiosity, to the next paragraph, but it certainly won't create interest that can be sustained by the proposition.

Here are some openings that do:

You are about to make a pleasant discovery!

That was the start of a letter used by a manufacturer of texture paint, to interest home owners in making ugly walls beautiful again. The letter went on to point out how even unsightly walls with cracks, faded paper, or rough spots can be made attractive again with this amazingly effective and easy-to-put-on plastic paint.

* * *

Suppose someone offered to install
in your home a $15,000 organ

This was used by a manufacturer of organs and sent to funeral homes. The second and third paragraphs went on to create desire by saying: "and place at your disposal the finest artists to play whatever pieces you wanted, whenever you wanted them . . . and offer to do all this at much less than 10% of the cost of the organ itself. Wouldn't that look like a pretty fine bargain?"

* * *

Does your group need money?

The first paragraph went on to develop the idea, as follows: If your club or society can use $100 or more, and it probably can, I'm going to make it possible for you to earn that much and more, with very little effort and no outlay of money.

* * *

How many customers are you losing each week?

* * *

Whether you believe in numerology or not, here are three numbers that could easily mean a lot to your company.

* * *

Have you stood at the entrance of your driveway recently to get a visitor's-eye view of your home? Try it sometime.

* * *

Here's a money bargain!
You've probably read and heard about bargains in many things, but chances are you've never been offered a bargain in money.

* * *

I have good news for you!

The word "news" is always intriguing. Certainly anyone who read this opening would go on to find out what the "good news" was.

The interest is strengthened by the second short paragraph:

Your winter overcoat, at half the price you'd expect to pay for it, is all ready for you to wear.

* * *

Notice how the following openings awaken interest and lead the reader on to find out more:

Here's something that looks as if it would be the most successful idea we have ever used to get leads for new business.

* * *

Folks say that the three quickest ways of spreading news are telephone, telegraph, and tell-a-woman. But since you've just moved into this neighborhood, the news about Elite may not have reached you. So here it is—

* * *

If you plan to "pretty-up" your employee washrooms, would this FREE service help?

* * *

If you are looking for a means to reduce the cost of fuel oil deliveries and thereby increase your profits, the enclosed circular on "Newtype" Synplastic Fuel Oil Hose will interest you.

* * *

It took us almost seventy-five years to create a sensation such as this. It will take you but a minute to realize that the enclosed book will mean a bigger Christmas sales volume than you've ever had before!

* * *

On reliable authority, we have learned that wholesale coal prices will advance next Fall. Disquieting news—but there is a way to beat the rising market if you act now!

* * *

If this idea can help you sell one house—it would be worth looking into. The fact that it has helped others to sell many houses would indicate that you too might use it to advantage.

* * *

This letter is in answer to the man who, one stifling hot day last July, said, "I'd give my eye teeth for a suit of clothes that would enable me to laugh at summer."

*   *   *

The enclosed announcement, while designed primarily for insurance agents, might also prove extremely interesting to *you*.

*   *   *

For two very good reasons, I am reminding you that a longer period than is considered safe has passed since we last examined your eyes.

*   *   *

Here's good news—a smaller, lighter, better hearing aid for about 50% less than the price of any comparable instrument.

*   *   *

Wouldn't you be interested in a larger share of good health than you've been enjoying recently?

*   *   *

Would you mind a personal question? The answer is really none of our business but is extremely important to you.

*   *   *

Here's the biggest *something for nothing* you've ever received—and we solemnly promise that there are no strings attached.

*   *   *

You and I are in the same boat—we're both looking for new business—and because we have a common objective, perhaps this proposal will interest you.

* * *

May I have just a few of your busy minutes, to request a favor?

* * *

Here's a crisp, new one dollar bill for you—for just one minute of your time.

* * *

Forgive me for starting this letter by telling you something you already know, but it bears repeating—

* * *

Here's an expert for your staff, but NOT for your payroll!

* * *

The right opening must be based on personal interest. You can be reasonably sure that the first paragraph of your letter will be read in any event, but the second and third and the rest of the letter will be read only if you ring the bell with your opening gun.

There are various kinds of ammunition available to you— the gain appeal, bargain appeal, sex appeal, pride appeal, emotional appeal, and others. Those which are directed toward the natural desire for gain and those which have a tendency to stimulate the emotions have generally proved to be the most effective. It has been my experience, however, that each problem stands pretty much by itself. The appeal to use in your opening is one that you feel will make the prospect anxious to read on, one that will arouse the kind of interest you can sustain in the following paragraphs.

The opening is your opportunity to guide the thoughts of your prospect into the proper channels. It is the way-paver for your proposition, the advance guard that makes receptive the mind of your reader.

CHAPTER FOUR

Writing the Body

First let's review the letter formula: Interest—Desire—Conviction—Action.

The first of these we take care of in the opening paragraph. The next two belong in the body of the letter, and the fourth in the close.

The second paragraph, therefore, is usually a continuation of the thought expressed in the first and the start of an attempt to create desire. Here we want to show the prospect what the product or service will do for him, rather than enter into a discussion of what the product is and how it works. Many sales letters make the mistake of assuming that the real story lies in a description of the product. It doesn't; the only thing the prospect is interested in is *what the product will do for him*. Never forget that, because it is extremely important.

Let's take an example. The first paragraph of a letter to car owners reads as follows:

What would you say if someone suddenly stopped you and asked—"What is it that everyone wants plenty of?"

The question was then answered—

You'd come right back with a snappy "Money, of course." And you'd be absolutely right.

Notice how easily you find yourself in the second paragraph, which reads—

Let's assume that you, then, would welcome the opportunity to add to your income. Especially if you could do it with practically no effort and without interfering in any way with what you are now doing to make a living.

Then came the clincher—

That's exactly what you can do through the Million Dollar Car Wax Plan.

Now, it is time to whet the appetite further and start building believability in the idea. Here comes the next paragraph—

As you read the other side, you'll see that almost unlimited earnings can be yours through this plan. But that isn't all there is to it—

We all like a good-looking car. But most of us hate like the dickens to hand out $15 every so often to have it waxed and polished. Well, why do it when you don't have to? Why pay $15 when you can do the job yourself with very little effort, for only $1! You can, that is, if you use Million Dollar Car Wax—

It produces a beautiful, high gloss polish with practically no effort at all. You just put it on—let it dry, then wipe it off. That's all there is to it.

Yes, you not only save money, but you do a professional-looking job of cleaning, waxing and polishing your car all in one operation. That's saving time as well as money.

As you can see, the first job is to sell the reader on the value of the wax itself. The next step is to show how this wax can be a means of additional earnings—

Now read the other side. Then, when you're through, lose no time in acting because the sooner you act, that much sooner your extra earnings will start coming in. Another thing—the sooner you act, the *bigger* those extra earnings will be. Mail the order form right now.

The other side of the letter was devoted to a complete description of the plan itself.

Here's a case where we are selling not a product, but an idea—the idea that good music develops character and that to have good music you should have a good piano.

Wouldn't you like to know what kind of an adult your child will grow up to be?

It's hard to tell, when they are young, just what life has in store—and for that reason it is difficult to train them along lines leading to a definite goal.

We do know, however, that success depends largely upon character—and character can certainly be developed right from the cradle!

One important way of teaching character is by encouraging good habits. Opening the child's eyes to the beauties in life is another.

And heading the list of things that are beautiful is music. It reaches the soul of a child—gently moulds thoughts that broaden character.

It all leads to this: you can help your child grow— *inside*—by affording the advantages of a musical education. He—or she—can learn best by *doing*. Let the youngster find pleasure and satisfaction and friendliness in ivory keys and restful music.

You'll never regret the day you first sat your child at a new piano. You will be placing *power* in that young one's hands—power to attain depths of understanding that help immeasurably in attaining future happiness.

First paragraph—*interest,* in the form of curiosity as to what is to follow. Second, third, and fourth paragraphs, continuing the thoughts expressed in the first and at the same time creating a *desire* through the discussion of Character. Fifth, sixth, and seventh paragraphs, the building of *Conviction,* that a musical education is important in the life of every child—then the tie-in with the piano (the instrument being sold) and finally the *action,* which paragraphs have been omitted.

Following is a letter that skillfully discusses the benefits to be derived by the reader.

The chances are you could buy a pair of silk stockings every week with the saving that Elite's new "25 pieces for $1.10" plan offers you.

Or an extra trip to the movies, a Christmas Fund ... but then, no one has to be told what to do with *extra money.*

The thing to consider is that extra money is waiting for you ... thru this economy service that washes, irons and delivers—*within 2 days*—twenty-five pieces, flatwork and as many as a dozen pieces of wearing apparel, for only $1.10—that's less than five cents each. (Additional pieces are charged for at four cents.)

The Elite Laundry, with considerably more than a quarter of a century of experience, is in an ideal position to give you the utmost for your laundry dollar, as this new plan proves.

Why not, this week, give it a trial? So many women have adopted it since we first wrote you, and are delighted with the service, that we feel sure you will be too.

Put the enclosed card in the mail ... our driver will call any day you say and in *two days* your clothes and linens will be back all ready to be put away.

P.S. Another reason for Elite preference is the fact that we use *Zeolite Water Softener*. Every woman knows what soft water means in washing.

Here's another good letter that follows closely the sales-letter formula:

What are you "fishing" for business with—what kind of bait?

Prospects today don't seem to be biting on the usual stuff at all. We have a retail store here in York, so we know from experience.

But give them something attractive, something that appeals to *everyone*, SOMETHING FOR NOTHING, and instantly the fishing for business gets better.

We know that from experience, too, for we have talked personally with dealers who are really using the Weaver Verti-Mignon Prize Contest. They tell us there is a distinct psychological advantage in being able to offer prospects the chance to get the piano of their choice entirely free.

They tell us they are closing prospects who didn't expect to buy for several months. They tell us their prospects are buying *better* pianos, spending more for them, in order to get in on the Prize Contest.

Why pass up such attractive "bait"—when it is so certain to get results? You wouldn't do that if you really were fishing. You'd use the bait that the fish wanted. You'd use the bait that got "strikes."

That's exactly the kind offered by the Weaver Prize Contest, and while the contest marches on there is still time to get in some very profitable "fishing."

Notice the continuity in this letter, sent out by a manufacturer of equipment used in electrotype plants:

May we tell you about something that has proved extremely profitable in our own plate-making department—and *can be just as profitable in yours?*

Innumerable experiments with various stereo casting methods have led to the development of The Westcott & Thomson Patented Vacuum Casting Box. Please do not confuse this with any other vacuum casting box. It is distinctly our own design, embodying precision qualities unequaled by any other similar unit.

We are using a whole battery of them now, in our own commercial plate-making plant, with great success. Many are in satisfactory operation in other plate foundries as well—all over the country. Everybody agrees . . . and you will too . . . that we've topped every casting method known from every standpoint.

The inside pages of the enclosed folder will tell you more about it. You will be particularly interested when I tell you that you can increase both speed and efficiency in your own shop without a necessarily large investment. Westcott & Thomson Patented Vacuum Casting Boxes are so priced that they literally *pay for themselves* in added profit on every job. And that's a promise!

We make other promises, too. Turn to the folder now and read about them. Then, for information about the specific box you need, mail the enclosed card.

This letter was designed to locate prospects for a local piano store. Note how easy it is to read, how you are literally *drawn* from one paragraph to the next. That's *suction*.

May we send you a piano—FREE?

Not a big one, of course, but a perfect little ivory plastic piano that we'd like you to have as a gift, if you don't already own a real piano.

This beautifully designed, miniature concert grand is just 3¼″ tall and you'd never guess it's a savings bank too. It looks so real you can easily imagine pixie fingers gliding over the plastic keyboard while rhythmic feet work the tiny pedals. Behind the music rack where no one would suspect, there's a slot where any size coin slides out of sight. It's a decorative miniature which your children will want for their very own.

Children love pianos—even a make-believe one—because in their imaginations they do everything a grown-up does. Playing a piano, being the center of gaiety and song, is a dream few children miss. What a wonderful thing to give your child the opportunity to make that dream come true!

A fine piano brings music into your home. But equally important, in learning to play, your child gains confidence and poise, develops a love and appreciation of music that grows with the years. No talent is more prized than the ability to play the piano.

We chose a miniature grand piano as your gift because of the fame of the Lester Grand. This superb instrument was just selected above all others as the official piano of the Philadelphia Orchestra.

The craftsmen who build the Lester Grand, designed and perfected the moderately priced Betsy Ross Spinet so that everyone could own a truly fine piano. It is a beautiful instrument with a magnificent tone, available in modern and traditional styles, and in many sizes—even for the smallest room.

Of course, none is as small as the exquisite ivory miniature we want to send you as a gift. But our supply is limited so please mail the enclosed card *today*. There will be no cost or obligation of any kind.

Conviction

Another essential requirement of a letter is that it be *believed*. It isn't enough that it just be read. After reading, the prospect must be in a frame of mind to accept the statements and claims as being absolutely true.

This you can accomplish by backing up the statements you make with facts to prove them, by making only statements that are not apt to be challenged or doubted, and by the sincerity you are able to put into your words.

You can usually tell at a glance when a letter lacks *believability*. When you are through reading, there is a big question mark in your mind. You're hovering somewhere between flat refusal to accept the claims and slight skepticism, which is almost as bad because you still won't buy if you're not sold on the idea that it is to your advantage to do so. To illustrate lack of believability, I can't help quoting from a sign I saw in the window of a very dingy-looking restaurant in one of the poorer sections of Philadelphia:

America's finest dinner

$.75

This is gross exaggeration, of course, but you'd be surprised how many letters are guilty of the same crime in varying degrees.

The experienced letter writer, even before he puts pencil to paper, will come to some conclusion in his own mind about the probable mental attitude of the prospect. Will he be receptive to the proposition? Will he be indifferent to it? Only by anticipating the answers can you achieve the very necessary quality of *believability*.

Here's a letter, the statements in which no reader would question:

Did you ever see a *real* sheik?

We don't mean the tea-drinking kind, but the white-robed, bearded sheiks of the Desert that you find in French Northern Africa.

If you'll come with us on this ideal Mediterranean Cruise . . . sail on the Homeric—"The Ship of Splendor" —with a selected group of the type of people you'd like to know . . . you'll see many even more fascinating things than an African Sheik.

You'll be thrilled to the tip of your toes . . . for there's Jerusalem, the Riviera, the great Casino at Monte Carlo, the Alhambra, Cadiz, Tunis, the newly excavated ruins of Carthage, Vesuvius and Naples, the Baker's shop in Pompeii (remember your Caesar?), Athens and literally hundreds of strange, exotic scenes to add colorful history to your own autobiography.

There's a 72-page illustrated book on Thos. Cook & Sons Cruise to the Mediterranean and one copy has been laid aside for you. Won't you request it on the enclosed card? It's free, of course.

Here's a letter in which possible skepticism is offset by the guarantee of a reputable company:

Are you a slave
to your price tags?

Do you waste valuable time writing out your prices every morning, attaching them to pins and puncturing tasty cuts of meat?

McArthur Porcelain Price Tag Holders can end all that for you. THEY'RE PERMANENT. They stay where you put them, *where the customer can see them,* and they don't have to be anchored in any way! Never before was there an easier or more effective way to price meats and delicatessen specialties.

The holders are made of metal with a sparkling white porcelain finish. They are both good looking and durable. When you have McArthur Holders lined neatly along your shelves and inside or in front of platters, they look like a part of your equipment and add to the attractiveness of your display. The smooth porcelain and laminated slides are easy to clean and keep clean.

There are two different kinds of McArthur Holders and you'll want some of each. No. 1 is for meat case shelves. The name of the product and the price are at an angle to extend over the rim of the shelf. This style is perfect for all cold cuts and delicatessen specialties which should not be priced with a stick-in tag. Style No. 2 is perfect for the lower part of your cases where fresh meats are displayed, because the price tag is flush with the surface. Two separate products can be marked in a single platter with this style.

Over 15,000 McArthur Porcelain Price Tag Holders are already in use and every day more and more grocers are using them to save time in pricing and to give products an appealing display.

Because we are so confident you will like this new idea in pricing, we will gladly send you any quantity of McArthur Price Tag Holders on a trial basis.

Try them for seven days and if you're not completely satisfied, simply return them and you'll owe us nothing.

The price of the holders includes the laminated slides for the various items and prices. You can easily see this is a worth-while investment that will save you time and help to sell more merchandise. Check and mail the order form today—*you'll be glad you did!*

One more example to illustrate the point, in which *believability* is helped by the sincere way in which the letter is phrased:

> May we add our congratulations to those of your family and friends, on your recent marriage?
>
> You'll say, of course, that we are a bit selfish in our interest, for obviously a new family just starting out means a new prospect. But, seriously, we want to help.
>
> If we can be *genuinely* helpful the *first* time you buy a rug or carpet—you'll come to us right through to your golden wedding anniversary!
>
> So won't you give us the opportunity to *prove* our sincerity—to point out to you from our complete stock of Hardwick & Magee Company rugs and carpets those which exactly fit your needs, your rooms, and your budget?
>
> It's amazing what a few carefully selected rugs or carpets will do to give you a head start in furnishing a home. And for finances—well, we know the problems facing a new family.
>
> Come in—won't you? You'll be mighty welcome, and pleased too, with our unusually fine assortment of rugs and carpets.

Personality

Another word for it is *naturalness,* that quality of a letter which knocks down the bars of resistance and puts you on friendly terms with the writer. A letter that has personality unconsciously makes you "warm up" to whatever proposition it contains. Whether you respond or not, you feel as though you'd like to. Your reaction is one of friendliness for the person (or company) who wrote it. You feel that the writer was absolutely sincere in whatever he said. Here's a letter that has personality even though it is obviously a circular letter:

It's a wonderful sight!

Did you ever watch a child's expression as she finishes her first tune on the piano?

There's a mixture of pleasure and pride, a dash of surprise, and a new look of confidence that wasn't there before. The thrill of accomplishment opens up a whole new horizon.

All children are born with a song in their hearts and, if you help them express that song on the piano, your children are destined for a happy future. Piano study fosters a love and appreciation of music that brings hours of contentment. It's a character builder in the formative years, develops confidence and poise. Many a timid child has gotten a new lease on life because of the ability to play. It makes for leadership at home and at school, adds to the popularity of every child and grownup.

Today more people than ever are realizing the importance of making a piano a part of their family life. It's the most musically complete of all instruments. Teen-agers find an outlet for excess energies. Adults turn an ordinary evening into one of companionable jollity and song.

The Betsy Ross Spinet makes it possible for everyone to own a fine piano. The master craftsmen who build the famous Lester Grand, now the official piano of the Philadelphia Orchestra, have designed a beautiful, small, moderately priced piano with a magnificent tone. And there are many styles to add warmth and character to any type of room.

So that you can visualize a Lester in your home, we've prepared a brochure showing ten different room settings. May we send you a copy at no obligation? Just drop the enclosed card in the return mail.

This letter has personality simply because it is so naturally written:

May we tempt you this morning with a free copy of the latest Winston Universal "Graphic Dictionary"?

As you may have guessed, it's not an easy job for an outside printer to get even a "look in" with some of the larger agencies like your own. Yet from your standpoint, there is every reason why we should be doing some of your work.

Certainly there couldn't be any question about QUALITY for we've been doing fine work for more than 30 years—have plenty of specimens to prove it.

And certainly we have the advantage when it comes to PRICE and SERVICE. When a publisher has learned to turn out literally millions of books at a profit, he *must* of necessity be geared up to economically print folders, booklets, broadsides, catalogs, etc.

DAY AND NIGHT operation of our presses assures prompt delivery with no extra charges for overtime—*an important point!*

We should like to make it worth your while to listen, for not more than ten minutes, to the rest of the story—hence this suggestion that you let us present you with one of our finest self-pronouncing dictionaries (1152 pages—size 5½" x 7⅞") in return for your courtesy.

What do you say—a fair exchange? Put the card in the mail and tell us a convenient time.

We—Our—Us

One of the biggest obstacles to the achieving of personality in a letter is a wrong balance in the use of personal pronouns. Hence we must avoid leaning too far in either direction. You've seen many letters in which "we," "our," and "us" seem to stick out everywhere. That is wrong because you're telling the story entirely from your side of the fence, whereas the prospect is interested in *himself* and what you can do for him.

You have also seen letters where the writer has bent over backward the other way. The "you" becomes conspicuous, and that is wrong because it seems to rob the message of all sincerity.

The proper balance in personal pronouns results in a "you-and-I" type of letter, which inspires the reader-across-the-desk-from-the-writer feeling that builds confidence. The point is this: Don't talk entirely about *your* idea or product, and don't talk entirely about *his* problem and needs. Link the two together.

Example of selfish writing

Gentlemen:

We are one of the largest processors of Western Red and Northern White Cedar poles, posts, ties, fencing, pulpwood and lumber in the United States and we are desirous of expanding our Fencing Division throughout the United States and through dealers and distributors.

Our company is a forty-eight-year-old institution with general offices located in Chicago, Illinois.

We manufacture a complete line of arbors, trellises,

children's play cabins, picket fencing, stockade fencing, rail fencing, ranch style fencing, and flower bed & corner fencing in various heights with gates to match. We have a complete Advertising and Sales & Installation program.

We manufacture a quality line of fencing and you will find our prices are very competitive. We do not anticipate any problems in filling our dealers' and distributors' fencing requirements as we own considerable cedar lands from which we obtain raw material for our products. Our raw material and products were not rationed during World Wars One and Two.

Our franchise is exclusive. Our products have sales appeal—require no servicing and carry a very substantial mark-up.

If you are capable of organizing or now have a retail sales organization, we would welcome an opportunity to present our Sales Program to you, without obligation.

Wire or write for the facts.

> Yours very truly,

Now get out your blue pencil and go to work.

Underline the selfish or bragging sentences.

Circle the *we-our-us* pronouns in red, the *you* pronouns in black.

Count each group and compare.

Reread the story on Sales Letters and appraise this letter with the sales-letter formula in mind.

It doesn't stack up, does it?

CHAPTER FIVE *Writing the Close*

W_e are now concerned with that part of the letter which has to do with the actual landing of the "fish." It's one thing to choose the proper bait, take it to the right place, and bring your catch up to the boat. It's something else to really land him. Some of the biggest fish ever hooked jumped back into the water a split second before they were caught. At least that's what the fishermen tell us.

Sending out letters to get inquiries or orders is something like fishing, certainly to the extent that "nearums" don't count. You *must* get your prospects to respond before your investment can yield a return.

The letter that arouses interest, creates desire, and builds confidence in the proposition, only to leave the prospect "hanging in mid-air" so far as a decision to act is concerned, isn't worth the paper it's written on. Authorities agree that a high percentage of the letters that fail can attribute their failure to a wrong closing paragraph. To put it another way, a *strong* close will many times double and even triple the returns obtained from a letter properly constructed in other respects.

You've seen letters produce good results although they didn't have a particularly strong close? Of course you have, and here's why:

The prospects for any proposition can be divided into three groups: (1) those who want what you have to sell and are literally *waiting to buy,* (2) those who *can be persuaded to buy* with the proper appeal, and (3) those who for one reason or another *can't buy,* no matter how attractive the proposition might be.

The prospects in Class 1 are naturally going to respond, even though the close in the letter may be weak. Those in Class 3 will not buy in any event, so you can forget them. And those in Class 2, the group to which every sales letter should be aimed, will not be moved to reply unless the letter follows the formula from start to finish and arouses interest, creates desire, inspires conviction, and urges *action*.

Types of Closers

There are quite a number of different kinds of closing paragraphs. There would have to be, because there are so many different kinds of letter objectives.

The Low-gear Type

For instance, one type of letter aims at nothing more than "keeping in touch" with the prospect or customer. The closing in this case is simply a graceful exit. When you're through saying what you've set out to say, you stop. That's the end of the letter because actually there's nothing specific you want the reader to do, at least at the moment.

A monthly letter to dealers winds up by saying:

> The Heller & Brightly guarantee that goes with every instrument we make is your assurance of complete satisfaction and years of dependable, accurate service.

A laundry's letter to housewives closed by saying:

> Our routeman will be around soon to give you complete information and to answer any questions that might be in your mind. Look for him.

A quality candy store sent a letter a month to a selected list of prospects. The following is typical of this type of close:

> Your letter, call, or visit to the store will be very welcome.

These are good paragraphs. Anything stronger would be decidedly in poor taste and fruitless in the bargain. Here's another of the same character in a letter used by a builder:

> The road to the home you would like to build can be made easy and pleasant. We are ready and able to help you.

The thought behind the whole appeal is that "whenever you're ready, it will be to your advantage to think of us." This kind of letter can't expect to get immediate results and doesn't attempt to. Hence, the closing paragraph is of the mild variety calculated to leave a good taste in the mouth rather than induce immediate action.

The Second-gear Type

Now come letters that require a little stronger type of close. They are not "high pressure" in any sense of the word, but they carry a little more urging than those just discussed.

One effective way of handling this situation is to end your story with a question, asking the reader point-blank if he won't take some kind of action. To illustrate:

> May we talk with you about *your* products, and the possibilities for increasing sales and profits? Just tell us a convenient time for a no-obligation interview. Use the convenient reply card enclosed.

Here are two more good closers of this type:

If you are interested in better results and a lower cost of operation, why not accept that challenge and order a few drums for test and comparison?

* * *

Since we are willing and glad to guarantee these same results in Diesel engines, don't you think it might pay you to order a few drums and see for yourself under your own conditions, just what M.H.S. can do for you?

The following closing paragraph combines the question with a statement that strengthens the request and lends weight to the argument already presented. It was in a letter selling surfboards to retail sporting-goods buyers:

Why not send us a small order and try them out? You won't be risking much and we feel confident you'll find them both fast moving and profitable.

This one, in a letter about a suburban development, is of the same kind:

Why not call Germantown 1246 now and let us take you there and back? Decide after you know ALL the facts and have seen ALL the advantages.

Another close of the second-gear variety is one that ends with a definite and rather strong statement. We are still not in the category of pressure closing. No return card is enclosed, and the letter will not be entirely judged on the basis of immediate results. What we are trying to accomplish may take ten or a dozen follow-up letters, yet we want to make each as productive as possible. The last two paragraphs of a follow-up letter to a prospective dealer illustrate a close that is frequently effective in cases of this kind:

With that in mind, please compare the LOVEKIN, point by point, with any other heater on the market, regardless of price.

If you do that, we feel quite sure you'll agree to the tremendous possibilities in the LOVEKIN LINE for an increase both in profit and load.

Here's another statement-type close that is as strong as it can be under the circumstances:

A suggestion from you that your patient investigate this new triumph of science would be appreciated by everyone concerned.

Here is still another, to make sure that you understand the type and the situations wherein it is appropriate:

The attached folder discusses cost and furnishes a convenient way of requesting complete information.

The High-gear Type

Letters sent out to get inquiries or orders, on the other hand, *must* induce action if they are to be productive. Their success or failure is judged entirely by the number of replies that come in and the sales that result. This kind of letter can't have any wishy-washy close. It cannot merely make a graceful exit. Nor can it leave the prospect in any doubt as to what you want him to do. It must be both urging and convincing, so that the prospect will not only have an easy, convenient way to reply but a logical, common-sense *reason* for replying.

To illustrate:

It has so many exclusive features and advantages that we can't possibly tell you about them in a letter, but if you'll return the enclosed card, we'll see that you receive

complete information—and without the slightest obligation of any kind. As a first step toward a more profitable
business, put your request in the mail today.

Step by step the reader was led through interest, desire, and
conviction to definite action. "Put your request in the mail
today."

In a letter whose objective was selling the prospect on the
idea of requesting a booklet, this very effective close was used:

You want to keep abreast of the times, of course, and
whether you can use this plan to advantage or not, at least
you'll want to know about it.

Fill in and return the card today and the booklet will
be put in the return mail.

Notice the *reason* for replying—"You want to keep abreast
of the times, . . . at least you'll want to know about it."

Here are some more closers that include reasons as well as
bids for action:

We're all ready for you . . . any day you say. Fill in
and return the enclosed card or call Stevenson 5823.
You'll soon find Elite's new 2-day plan saving you both
time and money.

* * *

Return the enclosed request for information card and
we'll be glad to show you how you can install a new
standard conditioned-air system, have all the advantages
of perfect refrigeration *and at the same time save money!*

* * *

If you'll request it, I'll be very glad to send you one of
these books. It will take you about six minutes to read

and might well be worth many hundreds of dollars in increased sales.

* * *

What do you say—a dictionary for a 10-minute interview—fair exchange? Put the card in the mail and tell us a convenient time.

* * *

Put the card in the mail now while you're thinking about it and we'll send you the catalog immediately—free and without the slightest obligation. Don't put it off . . . the sooner you get started, the sooner you'll have the specialized knowledge that commands a good salary.

* * *

We're only able to take care of a few more shirt manufacturers under the special Sperber service. So don't delay. Be sure you're not missing an opportunity to operate more economically. Mail the questionnaire *today* and be sure to include your patterns if you wish prices.

CHAPTER SIX *How to Make a Letter Productive*

A letter has the best chance of producing satis-factory returns when there has been put into it a *motive* for accepting the proposition it contains.

People, as a general rule, don't do things in this world just because we ask them to. If you doubt that, stop a stranger on the street sometime and say, "Would you be good enough to come around to my office tomorrow morning?" If you were that stranger, wouldn't you be inclined to say, "Why should I?"

If you tell a prospect how marvelous your machine is and what fine materials and workmanship have gone into its mak-ing, *but neglect to tell what the machine will do for him,* you can't really blame him for not being interested. By not telling him what your machine can do for him, you failed to supply a motive for accepting your proposition—and therein lies the secret to a good many hundreds of letter failures. Letters with-out a motive can sell but one class of prospects—the fellows who will buy no matter what you tell them, because they want what you're selling. As was pointed out in a previous chapter, every letter should aim at the prospects who are a challenge, those who say, in effect, "Come sell me. I'll buy it if you make me want it."

There are six predominating motives which, if properly

used, will unlock the door of a prospect's interest and induce him to act. Every successful speech, letter, sales talk, or sermon contains one or another of these same motives:

1. The desire for a profit or saving
2. The desire for comfort, pleasure, or convenience (self-indulgence)
3. The desire for protection of life, health, property, or interest
4. The desire to play fair (loyalty, courtesy, obligation, etc.)
5. The desire to own (pride of possession)
6. The desire to be popular

Analyze any letter that has produced good results, any speech that has "gone over with a bang," any sales talk that has proved its ability to get the name on the dotted line, or any sermon that has kept the congregation awake—and you'll find at least one of these six motives.

When someone tells you to write from the other fellow's viewpoint, what he really wants you to do is to give your readers a motive for accepting your proposition.

Right here, let me differentiate between a *reason* and a *motive*. When I say "motive for accepting your proposition," I mean something deeper and closer to the human emotions than just a cold, matter-of-fact reason. We must have reasons for doing things, of course, but, even with reasons, we don't do them without motives. It is by means of the appropriate motives that we are able to arouse the first spark of interest, fan it into a flame of desire, keep it alive with the fuel of conviction, and finally crash through with a blaze of action. It will pay you to be thoroughly familiar with all the different motives so that you can use them as good judgment dictates.

Following is an appeal to motive No. 1—the desire for a *profit:*

> Here's a crisp, new one dollar bill for you.

No, there are no strings attached. It's yours to keep. You may put it in your pocket right now if you wish. It is simply a token payment for your kindness in reading this letter, which brings important news about an opportunity I don't believe you will want to miss. To put it briefly:

We'd like to set up in your plant, *at our own expense,* a modern paging and broadcasting system which will not only enable you to locate anyone in your entire plant instantly—it will also provide your employees with music while they work—*all this for a 30-day trial period, without cost or obligation to you.*

We are willing to do this so that you can see for yourself, right in your own plant, how profitable a scientifically planned program of recorded music can be in a plant like yours.

You've probably read some of the amazing stories on the use of music in industry during the war—how it increases over-all efficiency, reduces errors, rejects and plant accidents, how it improves morale, cuts absenteeism, reduces job turnover. *It has been proved conclusively that music in industrial plants ups production six to eleven per cent!*

Remember, this trial installation costs you nothing. At the end of the trial period, if you feel that industrial music is not practical for you, we'll simply remove our equipment and there will be no obligation whatever. But I'm convinced that like thousands of other leading industrialists, you will want to keep music working for you. And I think you will be agreeably surprised at the moderate cost. There's no big investment to make, just a low monthly service charge.

If you will return the enclosed card, we'll get in touch with you immediately to arrange for the free trial installation.

This letter is of exactly the same type. Notice the strong appeal to the *profit* motive:

AN INTERESTING FACT

ABOUT PROFIT

The difference between a profitable and an unprofitable dining room operation is often the slight difference in *how* meals are served.

Experience has shown that the best patronized dining rooms have two features in common: *service* is prompt and courteous; the *atmosphere* is *pleasing*. Fortunately, creating the right atmosphere can be *profitable* for you, as well as pleasant for your guests.

We'd like to send you a *free* copy of a new handbook titled "SET TO SELL"—a complete, idea-filled guide to creating an attractive dining room at lowest possible cost.

"SET TO SELL" can show you how to gain smoother, quieter, more efficient service . . . how to add a cheerful, decorative touch of color to your dining room.

It will also show you the *profit* possibilities—how you can save on laundry expenses; cut linen replacements; speed up your service.

A copy of "SET TO SELL"—just off the presses—has been reserved for you. We know you will find it helpful and well worth having. Just fill out and mail the postage-paid reply card and we'll put it in the return mail. Why not do it now while the card is right before you?

The example below is an unusual application letter that uses the same profit motive:

I am not looking for a position!

No ordinary job will be even considered. I want to undertake what you may consider a seemingly impossible task—that of increasing your profits in the face of vicious price and service competition.

If you've had an unsatisfactory earnings and dividend record during the past five or six years, if your sales have been decreasing and you've been selling most of your plant output at no profit—then I respectfully apply for the back-breaking, full-time job of turning red ink into black.

Because of a rather exceptional background and a thorough understanding of those principles of manufacturing which govern pricing, selling and profit, I can determine for you—

1. Your minimum net profit requirement
2. The correct selling price for each product
3. Proper costs for production, plant operation and management
4. The proper quantity discounts
5. And the procedure and expenditure necessary to insure disposal of your normal output *at prices that will earn the predetermined profit requirement*

If these things are at all interesting to you, we can discuss them more in detail and more satisfactorily, in a personal interview.

Won't you set a convenient time?

A twin to the profit motive is the *saving* motive, and the two are so close in character that we class them together. Notice how the idea is brought out in the following letter, how it talks *saving* in the very first sentence.

Here's proof that we can *CUT YOUR SHIPPING COSTS!*

With everything to gain and nothing to lose, we want you to try out the new A.T.A. Motor Carrier Directory—entirely *at our expense.*

The A.T.A. Directory gives you up-to-date, accurate information on every phase of motor freight shipping—how to do it, whom to contact, the best routes, etc. It's clear, specific, easy to follow. But that isn't all—

—It is the only directory that gives at a glance both origin and destination points for more than 200,000 direct routes throughout all 48 states.

—It is the only directory issued under policies controlled by the American Trucking Association, Inc.; *therefore the only one sponsored by the motor carriers themselves.*

This unique motor freight guidebook was designed specifically to make freight routing easier, quicker and less expensive.

It has proved indispensable in busy shipping departments all over the country and I feel positive it can save time and money for you, too.

That's why I hope you will accept this offer of a free trial copy. We have one reserved for you now and if you'll just fill in and return the enclosed card, we'll send it off by return mail. It will be yours to use for 30 days on all your routing assignments—at no cost whatever.

At the end of the trial, if you don't agree that it would

be one of the best investments you could make, simply return it to us. There's no obligation. If you decide to keep it, you'll also receive the privilege of a year's FREE MAIL CONSULTATION SERVICE for any special problems that arise.

We believe sincerely that it will pay you to mail the postage-free reply card TODAY.

This letter to a selected list, sent out by a manufacturer of hosiery, presents the same point in an interesting manner:

Merry Christmas—and a timely reminder that you and the girls in your office can actually buy more Christmas presents for your friends for less money than last year . . . even in these inflation times!

. . . and lovelier gifts, too . . . gifts your friends regard as the most useful and appreciated of all—exquisite, luxury-sheer nylon hosiery—TEL-A-FREND Nylons, of course! (And what girl ever has too many?)

You can actually purchase *3 pairs* of beautiful top-quality, gift-quality TEL-A-FREND Nylons for less than the price of *2 pairs* purchased elsewhere, just by using the TEL-A-FREND GROUP PURCHASE PLAN.

Pass around our hosiery folder to the girls in your office and let them read about the amazing new feature in TEL-A-FREND Nylons that makes them softer, silkier, less fragile, more comfortable. They'll see that they not only save money—they also get finer stockings.

And here's a new pink form to make it easier for you to order. The idea is for each girl to write in what she wants, indicating style, quantity, etc. That tells you what to order from us—then the same form serves as a handy record of who gets what when the stockings arrive.

But please do get your TEL-A-FREND order in *now*. You

can make this a more-money-to-spend Christmas if you don't delay (and don't forget the shopping time everybody will save!). Be sure we'll fill your orders promptly.

Motive No. 2 appeals to the desire for comfort, pleasure, convenience, and other forms of self-indulgence, including the gratification of appetite, curiosity, etc. Here are two typical examples:

DAINTY VARIETY IN
YOUR MENUS WITH
THIS NEW FOOD!

Here's a new food—delicious, healthful, appetizing, and dainty. It will allow you to vary your menus and on top of that, will do more for you than any food you've ever eaten. Have you ever heard of Pecano? It's been tested and approved by *Good Housekeeping* and quite a number of stores are selling it, but it may be new to your neighborhood, and if so, you have a real treat ahead.

Pecano is a nutritious all-nut food (the result of a patented method exclusive to our Company). The choicest of fresh Georgia Pecans are so trans-shaped that they literally melt in your mouth. Nuts *made* digestible— that's what Pecano is—Nature's oldest, richest food transformed into a delicious, nourishing, easily digested food that can be served and eaten in hundreds of delightful ways.

SOMETHING NEW TO SERVE!

Most women are constantly on the lookout for new ideas for luncheon, tea and the regular daily menus— something different for the jaded appetite that every so often tires of sameness. Pecano is the perfect answer. Wait 'til you see the recipes that show how to make

Pecano Orange Bread, Pecano Butterscotch, Pecano Penuche, Pecano Apple Whip, Pecano Corn Loaf, Pecano Celery Croustades, Pecano Risotto—and there are eighty other tried and tested recipes for new and different kinds of bread, cake, candy, entrees, salads, sandwiches and desserts.

There's reason enough for trying Pecano, but there's so much more to say about this wholesome, natural food than just how good it is.

NOT ONLY DELICIOUS—HIGHLY NOURISHING, TOO!

Nuts generally have the reputation for being hard to digest. And they ARE. How often have you heard someone say, "I adore nuts, but they don't agree with me"? Scientific research has shown that countless small nut particles pass through the alimentary tract wholly indigested and this means not only distress but the loss of valuable nutrition.

In the invention of Pecano, science has completely solved this problem. It comes to you abounding in vitality-producing, body-building elements . . . a blood- and tissue-builder in wonderfully concentrated form . . . a delicious, natural food that gives you the benefit of high health value with little digestive effort. Pecano supplies valuable protein for building and repairing body tissues; natural nut oil for producing energy; food minerals, without which life cannot be sustained; and other vital elements essential to good health and resistance to disease.

The important thing about Pecano is that it contains the two great food essentials in proper ratio and in the purest, sweetest form. The proteins in Pecano are COMPLETE proteins, which means that in themselves they are sufficient to supply the full quota of tissue-building material.

Do you wonder thousands of women have adopted Pecano for everyday use—and call it the ideal food? Pecano is more than a table delicacy. It is a source of energy, "pep," vitality. It's convenient, easy and economical to use. There's no waste. It requires no cooking or preparing. Pecano is *all food*—ready to eat just as it comes.

SPECIAL TRIAL OFFER AND FREE RECIPE BOOK!

So sure am I that once you've tasted Pecano you'll fall in love with its rich, rare flavor and want it for *your* table —not only for its deliciousness, but for its health-building qualities—that I am going to make you a very special introductory offer. Pecano sells for $1.30 per pound—5 pounds for $6. If you'll send your trial order in promptly, I'll send you, postpaid, TWO POUNDS FOR TWO DOLLARS, and include without charge the 28-page book of delicious Pecano recipes.

Furthermore, if you're not entirely satisfied with your purchase, I'll refund your money any time within two weeks—without question. So many people are today using Pecano regularly—after having tried it as I want you to now—that I feel confident you'll soon be ordering the five-pound containers and serving this wholesome, tasty food on all occasions.

Put two one-dollar bills, or your check for two dollars, in the enclosed envelope. With *Good Housekeeping* and the better food stores all over the country recommending it, you can be sure that Pecano is all we claim for it.

My offer, however, only holds good if you send in your order promptly.

No postage is required for the self-addressed envelope —just fill out your request, enclose your remittance of $2 and mail.

Then be prepared for the TREAT OF YOUR LIFE!

This letter combines motive No. 1 and motive No. 2:

A DREAM THAT YOU CAN MAKE *COME TRUE!*

As a Summer Brook customer I want you to be one of the first to know about our new Silver Chinchilla Lapin Coats. I feel sure you'll be just as excited about them as we are.

Every woman dreams of having one truly beautiful fur coat in her wardrobe and this is a rare opportunity to make that dream come true.

For these coats, made from choicest pelts of Summer Brook's finest, scientifically bred Chin Chins have exceeded our highest hopes. We believe they are as rich looking and luxuriously beautiful as you'll see anywhere.

Look at the unretouched photographs in the enclosed folder and you'll understand why we are so enthusiastic. I know you'll agree that at their amazingly low price, they are a truly magnificent value.

Later on, we will of course make Silver Chinchilla Lapin coats and capes available to the general public. Right now, however, we are restricting their sale to customers and friends of Summer Brook Farm. We feel they should have the first opportunity to own one of these lovely furs—*and because you are a Chin Chin customer we offer them to you at a 10% discount from the regular list price.*

Just wait till your friends see you in one of these gorgeous coats or capes. Silver Chinchilla Lapin is really exquisite, flatteringly soft and lovely, yet surprisingly durable.

You can well understand that if these beautiful coats were available in a store, the list price would be a great deal higher. Because we are selling them direct, eliminating completely the middleman profits, our prices, considering beauty, quality and value, are unbelievably low.

And, think of it, *you* can buy one of these coats for 10% less than those already low prices listed in the folder! Furthermore, if it isn't convenient for you to pay cash, you may pay only one-third when the coat arrives, and the balance in six easy, monthly payments. You'll agree this is a very unusual opportunity, but remember we have only had a limited number of these coats and capes made up. I don't know how long it will take to get more when these are gone.

So don't put it off. Order yours today. Just fill in the enclosed form giving us the necessary information and your coat will be shipped to you immediately.

This letter illustrates an appeal to comfort, better living conditions—motive No. 2.

Wow! What a Christmas THIS Can Be!

What would you say to a Christmas present that gave you all this—

A more comfortable home, with no window drafts!

A year's supply of fuel every four years FREE!

Complete freedom from the dangerous, backbreaking job of putting up screens or storm windows twice every year!

Improved appearance and increased value!

You can enjoy these advantages, not only this year but

every year, simply by having us install HUNTER ALUMINUM COMBINATION STORM WINDOWS WITH INTERCHANGEABLE SCREENS. Can you think of a better gift for the entire family?

The enclosed folder will tell you some of the reasons why HUNTER WINDOWS are the most completely satisfactory on the market, thanks to a number of exclusive patented features not obtainable in any other window.

Remember, HUNTER WINDOWS are precision made, in the modern Hunter factory at Bristol, by craftsmen who do nothing else. And they are custom-fit to your particular windows. You will be dealing with an old established company, your installation supervised by men who pioneered in this business, and who have literally put in a quarter of a million combination windows.

You needn't make up your mind now. Let us give you a FREE DEMONSTRATION, right in your own home. Then if you've an eye for a smart investment (with *an average 17% return*) you'll say to our representative—"How soon can you put them in?"

The fact is—WE CAN MAKE ALMOST IMMEDIATE INSTALLATION. You'll have your HUNTER WINDOWS well before Christmas if you MAIL THE CARD NOW.

P.S. Self-storing screens are also available with HUNTER WINDOWS.

Motive No. 3 appeals to the desire for protection of life, health, property, or interest. The age-old motive of self-preservation is a powerful one. Whatever one's share of health and worldly goods, one wants to hang onto them. The motive in this case, therefore, may take the form of fear, however subtly expressed—fear that the life or health of loved ones may be in danger, that something which belongs to one may be in jeopardy or that all may not go well with some proposition in which one may be interested. Read the several letters that follow and see if you don't recognize motive No. 3 running through them:

A friend of mine is happier today than he has been for a long while. And he has reason to be.

For the first time since he and Mary were married—incidentally they have two small children—my friend says that he feels really comfortable about the future. If anything happens to him during the next 20 years, his wife will receive $100 a month for a full 20 years and then $10,000 in one lump sum.

A short while ago, such protection as that would have been far beyond his reach. Now, he can afford it easily, due to a new plan which my company is sponsoring and which no married man with children can afford to pass up.

The Plan needn't operate for 20 years. It can be 15 years, or 10. And it needn't be for $10,000—it can be much more or much less. It can be made to fit, *whatever* your protection requirements might be.

If you can possibly squeeze out a few dollars a week to buy security and peace of mind for your wife and boys (or girls or both)—you can take my word for it that you'll be very much interested in this unusual plan.

At any rate, I am going to phone you in a day or so and see if you won't let me tell you more about it.

* * *

At your convenience I should like to talk with you about a service for which there is no charge but which might easily be worth many thousands of dollars to you annually.

Perhaps I'd better say right at the outset that such men as Dr. Paul A. Smith, Dr. Arthur G. Jones, Jr., and Dr. Galen G. Brown, to mention just a few, have already used all or a part of this service of mine, to their definite profit and advantage.

Briefly, here's the way it works:

With increased efficiency and a more successful practice in mind, I first make a study of your internal management, office layout, method of handling patients and financial controls. Based on the findings, I then make specific recommendations, give you answers to such questions as you'll find on the sheet enclosed. Look over these questions carefully. You'll agree, I'm sure, that you MUST know the answers to them if you are to be of utmost value to yourself, your family and your profession.

The reason so many professional men consult me for the answers is because I have specialized for many years in internal management problems; estate, gift and income tax laws; public accounting; and insurance program analysis. The fact that I have helped them might suggest the possibility that I can also be of some help to you. At least, there is no cost to you or obligation of any kind attached to my trying.

Will you use the enclosed card to tell me a convenient time for an interview?

* * *

Don't read this letter if you can
say "yes" to just one question!
Can you afford to be sick . . . or have an accident?
If you can't, and most of us are in that class . . . then by all means take advantage of this special Health and

Accident Policy available to anyone between the ages of 16 and 70, male or female!

$10,000 worth of protection for
a full year for $10!

Anybody can afford $10 . . . none of us can afford, easily, the piling up of doctor's bills, medicines, etc., particularly when it's coupled with a temporary loss of income.

This is the new and improved Policy of the oldest and strongest Health and Accident Insurance Company in the world . . . which is in its 42nd year of successful business and has paid over 12 million dollars to sick and injured policy holders.

Read the enclosed folder carefully. See how completely it covers all the usual types of accidents and illnesses . . . then fill out the application and return it to us with check or money order.

We guarantee to refund the full amount if you are not satisfied with the policy after you have received it. So don't delay!

P.S. None of us expect to be sick . . . but then none of us really KNOW.

* * *

Motive No. 4 aims at the average person's normal desire to play fair and be loyal—his desire to fulfill a sense of obligation, courtesy, or honesty.

Notice motive No. 4 in these letters:

So many people shy away from so-called advertising letters that I hasten to say—this *isn't* one. It's a personal letter requesting information and I'll be very grateful to you if you'll give it to me.

We've just recently sent you a number of folders and samples of HOPEWELL KRAFT BOARD, a box material made of the same strong KRAFT so universally used for wrapping paper.

In these pieces, we discussed the fine savings available to you through its use—savings substantial enough to be interesting *anytime,* but particularly attractive NOW, when economies of all kinds are welcome.

This campaign, while highly successful in a general way, failed completely as far as you are concerned and I want to know if there's been any slip-up on our part.

Would you mind very much, simply as a business courtesy which I shall greatly appreciate, taking your pencil and jotting down the answers to a few questions listed on the reverse side of this letter?

Don't bother to dictate—just scribble your reply on the back and use the enclosed stamped envelope.

I hope some day there'll be some way of repaying your kindness . . . in the meantime, please accept our best wishes for a happy and prosperous year!

* * *

Please . . .
  some crippled children
  need your help

—and their need is desperate, urgent. Without you, there is no way to give them the expensive treatment that alone can make them well.

Buy Easter Seals and you make miracles possible!

Little children, helpless from cerebral palsy, learn to walk and talk again. The physically handicapped are given the chance they want so much to be more like other people—to be independent and earn their own way in life.

Your Easter Seal contributions maintain a school and summer camp for crippled youngsters—a workshop, training classes and a job placement service for the handicapped. I wish you could see with your own eyes what your kindness enables us to do. I know it would make you very proud.

Each year, we call on our friends for help and each year you respond generously. We're counting on you again this year. We have to because the annual sale of Easter Seals is our only source of funds for this important work.

I know that you will give as much as you possibly can. Just use the enclosed envelope to mail us your contribution check or cash. And accept our heartfelt thanks in advance for those you will be helping.

Best wishes for a happy Easter season.

* * *

Wouldn't you like to
BACK A BOY like this?

Besides the YMCA, the only place he has to grow up is the street. And, believe it or not, there are 5400 such boys within the area served by the central branch of the "Y."

These boys *need and want* what the YMCA can give them—the opportunity of becoming healthy, well-balanced, responsible citizens—and a Christian philosophy of living that will prepare them for a useful, purposeful life.

Will you help them get it?

The YMCA's program for youth isn't particularly dramatic. It doesn't concentrate on the 2% who are delinquent, but rather aims to provide good leadership and character education for the 98%, the constructive help so much needed everywhere today, especially in the mid-city area.

This is the time each year when we hold our PARTNER-MEMBERSHIP campaign. Please consider this, therefore, a friendly, hopeful knock on your door in behalf of YOUTH.

We have a bigger program and a bigger need in 1956 than ever before. But if we are to do more, for more boys, we need your generous support.

Won't you fill in and mail the enclosed PARTNER-MEMBERSHIP form today? We'll be very grateful, but more important—you will have the satisfaction of knowing that you have given a lift up to some very worthy youngsters.

P.S. Partner Memberships are issued in any amount from $10 up, are of course tax deductible, and may be paid for in quarterly or semi-annual installments if you prefer.

* * *

You have a right to know WHY—

As you know by now, the goal set by your Community Chest this year is higher than ever before. To attain that goal, we are asking you to give *more* than you generally give—if you possibly can.

In times like these, when we're all finding it so much more expensive to live, that must seem like asking a great deal. But this is work that *must* be done. And there is no other way but to ask this *extra* effort from you. First of all, however, you are entitled to know the facts.

I believe everyone has a pretty good general idea of what the Community Chest is and does. You know that it acts as collector for 170 different charitable and humanitarian agencies—that the annual Red Feather Drive is a concentration of scores of charitable solicitations into *one great united appeal.* But do you realize just how much vitally important work your Red Feather contribution performs? How many essential services it renders?

—it provides hospital care for those unable to pay for it by helping to support 26 Philadelphia hospitals.

—it sends competent registered nurses into the homes of the poor, supports 24 specialized Health Agencies in maintaining health, checking disease.

—it shelters little children without homes or families, provides day nursery care through its 33 Child Care Agencies.

—it trains our youth for good citizenship, teaches them to work and play together in recreation centers, in settlements, the Y's, the Boy and Girl Scouts.

—it teaches the handicapped a profitable trade, shelters the aged and homeless, aids runaway children and stranded travelers, provides legal counsel for the poor—through 20 specialized agencies.

You can well understand that the cost of so vast a work is great at any time. And now, when your dollar will buy only 60¢ worth of food, clothing, fuel, service, the cost is great indeed. But the price we would *all* have to pay if we *neglected* our obligations, would be much, much higher.

Philadelphia has always taken care of its own and we feel sure we can count on you *now,* in this year of crisis, to put this Red Feather drive over the top.

Motive No. 5 appeals to that part of a person's make-up which takes a definite pride in the ownership of something fine and which finds satisfaction in the maintaining of self-respect and in the building of reputation and prestige. That such things constitute real motives for action is elementary. What I want to do here is simply to make you conscious of them. Most of us *know* how vital it is to keep the old head down during a golf swing, but how easily and often we forget. Most of us know how vital motives are in the preparation of every letter, and yet how easy it is to sail right into an argument without at least one of them with us to insure success.

See if you can't see motive No. 5 between the lines of these examples:

> How much is your child's
> happiness worth to you?

There was a time when many parents who wanted to enrich their children's lives through piano study just couldn't afford to do so. A good piano was too expensive.

But things are different now. You can get a beautiful Lester Betsy Ross Spinet with a magnificent tone for literally just a few dollars a week.

What a small sum to pay to bring music and happiness into your home, to develop in your children an artistic gift that will add to their popularity and bring them lifelong contentment. Knowing how to play the piano, whether for your own enjoyment, for your family and friends, or for the concert stage, is one of the most treasured of all talents.

Many years ago, the makers of the famous Lester Grand Piano (recently chosen the official piano of the Philadelphia Orchestra) recognized the need for a moderately priced piano.

So, they set their experienced craftsmen to work, putting into a smaller piano the same important features and same fine materials found in their Grand Piano. The result is the Betsy Ross Spinet—a beautiful piano with exquisite tone—designed, styled and priced for the modern home.

May we send you a booklet telling more about the Lester Betsy Ross Spinet and Grand Pianos? Just mail the enclosed card today. There'll be no obligation, of course.

* * *

There's something mighty human and interesting about a man big enough to admit his shortcomings.

A successful man, controlling fifteen separate businesses and a large factory, says in his letter—"The Britannica has saved me, by sound advice, more than I paid for it." But it did more than that!

"It has taught me the wonder of a hobby and how to enjoy it. It has made smooth my home life by giving my wife and children knowledge obtainable at a moment's notice. It has opened up the world to me for travel.

"It has helped me to improve my education, enabling me to undertake public work. It has smashed to pieces any egotistical ideas of 'know-all' by illustrating the extent of my ignorance." And so on.

I don't believe any of us realize how little we do know until we have at our side, always available, the overwhelming number of facts comprising literally a summary of all the knowledge in the world.

It's a thrill to have the "answer to everything" so accessible and I'd certainly like you to have a taste of it. This time . . . won't you *use* the card?

P.S. No obligation and no annoyance. And don't forget the 40% saving.

* * *

It is interesting to note that very few socially undesirable people have an appreciation for music. The two are incompatible. Music—and particularly the ability to play —develops fine perceptions and sensitivities—builds and refines character.

Your child should have a musical education—for the youngster's own happiness! Interest in music keeps young minds—during leisure time—in pleasant, active channels. And what a feeling of satisfaction and accomplishment your child will get when he or she can speak professionally about a piano having "full tone" and "quick touch."

That's why it is important to start your youngster's musical education on a piano of which the child can always be proud—an instrument he or she can grow to love for its fine qualities, its sheer beauty of tone.

A Weaver instrument would be your child's selection if a musical knowledge was already developed. When you see one of these superb pianos, I am sure it will be your choice, too.

The care and enduring strength with which it has been built, the rich beauty of its lines make it stand out as an instrument of charming perfection—one that you will cherish always.

Here is a letter built around the desire to be popular, motive No. 6.

Congratulations—you have taken the first step toward increased social and business success!

That may sound like a pretty strong statement, but when you consider that your speaking voice reflects your personality, *controls the impression you make on everyone you meet,* it's easy to see how your voice can become your most powerful asset.

That's why we've entitled the enclosed folder "How to Win Business and Social Success through VOICE CONTROL." Read it carefully. Consider the many advantages that are yours, the poise and self-confidence you will acquire when your voice attracts and *holds* the attention of others.

Just the other day a student wrote me—"I begin my new show next week. No mention is ever made of my 'monotonous voice' now. I am deeply grateful for your voice lessons." We know of the radio success of this student. His voice has regained its youthful sparkle and his resulting success in radio has changed his whole outlook on life.

A young executive of a large business concern wrote "Your voice course is a continuous source of increasing helpfulness to me as a profitable self-improvement study. The records are outstanding in their method and long-time usefulness."

We are constantly receiving similar reports from our students everywhere—men and women in every type of business. Their success can be yours with this unique Home Study Course. Now, in the privacy and comfort of your own home you receive the same instructions given my private students here in our New York studio—*but at a fraction of the cost.* It's easy! It's fun! Just study each lesson, then play the records and listen while I demonstrate the points brought out. In no time at all, you'll notice improvement in your voice and its effect on others.

If you are sincere in wanting to make your voice a definite asset—if you want your spoken words to be more convincing, more forceful—then mail the enclosed enrollment blank today. You need send only $7.50 now, then only $5 a month for six months. That's all you pay for the complete set of instructions, including my book and the six records. If you prefer, you may send $32.50 now in full payment, thus saving $5. In either case you must be entirely satisfied, or you may return both book and records within 7 days for full refund of every dollar you paid.

But don't wait another minute to take this important step. Fill in and mail the enrollment blank TODAY.

* * *

Keep this very important point in mind—people aren't anywhere near as interested in the *thing* (product, service, or idea) you have to sell, as they are in *what it will do for them.* They'll buy, or act, for one or more of these basic reasons.

1. To make money
2. To save money
3. To save time
4. To avoid effort
5. To get more comfort
6. To achieve greater cleanliness
7. To attain fuller health
8. To escape physical pain
9. To gain praise
10. To be popular
11. To attract the opposite sex
12. To conserve possessions
13. To increase enjoyment
14. To gratify curiosity
15. To protect family
16. To be in style
17. To have or hold beautiful possessions
18. To satisfy appetite
19. To emulate others

20. To avoid trouble
21. To avoid criticism
22. To be individual

23. To protect reputation
24. To take advantage of opportunities

There are undoubtedly other appeals but these will serve at least to steer your thinking in the direction of your prospect.

CHAPTER SEVEN

Letter Problems

We've talked a lot about how letters should be written. Now let's *write* some, starting from scratch and carrying the job right through to the finished letter.

First, however, let's have a little review. We start, of course, with the assumption that you have something to sell—if not a product, a service or idea.

If you do, and it isn't convenient or economical to sell it through personal solicitation, a good letter (or series) will probably be your best selling medium.

Now that we've cleared the way, you're all ready to start on your letter.

Ready? Got a pencil and pad before you?

First thing, write down the kind of people who should be most interested in your product or service. Are they young or old—male or female—workers or white collarites—business or professional people—individuals or companies, etc.

Now write down the *features* of your product, in the order of their importance.

Next, *translate* those features into customer-benefits. For example, a good location may be a *feature,* but it isn't a *benefit* until it's translated into *convenience* and *time-saving.* Don't make your prospect do the translating—*you* do it.

Mark in some way the benefits you have listed that may be *news* to your prospect.

This isn't *all* the advance preparation needed, because you should also be fortified with *facts* to back up any *claims* you are going to make, proof of performance, success stories, etc. —but at least you are ready to get started.

Look over the list of *benefits* now, and select the one which will in your opinion create the greatest *stir,* arouse the greatest *interest,* be the one most certain to make your prospect *want to read on.* Write half a dozen short opening paragraphs, using the leader you've selected. Remember, the entire job of selling isn't accomplished in the first sentence or two, either by a letter or by a salesman. A person has to get *hungry* before he's ready to eat. It's your job to make him *hungry* for whatever you have to sell.

Chances are you won't get the *best* opener right away. *Keep writing opening paragraphs until you have one that you believe can't fail to click—with the particular kind of people on your mailing list.* This is the most important part of your letter. If it doesn't do its job, the other parts won't get a chance to do theirs.

Following are a few good interest-arousing paragraphs to illustrate the point:

> Here is a new plan that enables you to have more and more cash in your Savings account, a steadily increasing stack of U.S. Defense bonds, and extra Life Insurance— *all with one small weekly deposit.*

* * *

> Would you be interested in having $1,000 of additional Personal Accident Insurance, without having to put out one extra penny for it?

* * *

> Announcing a new IDEA—and I guarantee you'll like it!

* * *

If you don't read this letter now, you'll wonder all day what it says . . .

* * *

The measure of a good opener is the extent to which it *forces* the reader into the next paragraph, preferably through *interest* rather than just plain curiosity.

Okay—got a good beginning for your letter? Then let's go on—

Now that the prospect has pricked up his ears, capitalize on the interest you have aroused by following through with more benefits, or an elaboration of the one you opened up with. The function of the second (and perhaps third and fourth) paragraph is further to whet the appetite, to create a real desire for the product or service you are writing about.

Have you done that? Satisfied with what you've written? Then, let's proceed with the next part—building *believability*.

In the first paragraphs of your letter you have drawn a word picture, have promised certain benefits that the reader will enjoy as the result of your product or service if he buys. Now comes one of your toughest assignments—making him accept what you've promised as a likely possibility, convincing him that your product or service will really live up to the claims you've made. This part of the letter calls for PROOF.

What can you say to back up what you've promised? Any success stories? Testimonials? Case histories? Perhaps you don't need any of those things. It could be that the reputation of your company is in itself sufficient to establish confidence in anything you say or sell.

Assuming that you have fulfilled the first three requirements of a sales letter—*interest, desire, conviction*—you are ready to go after the desired *action*. If possible, don't just ask your prospect to send a card back for more information, or stop in at your store or bank—point out a reason why it is to *his* advantage to do what you ask—and *now,* not just any old time.

Here are two good action closers, just to give you an idea:

Financial security for you and your family need no longer be a dream. It can be yours now with the Packaged Saving Plan. Why not stop in this week?

* * *

After you have looked over the enclosed samples, make sure of prompt service by filling in and mailing the convenient order form today.

* * *

Now, let's look at some actual problems.

Problem No. 1. This is a comparatively simple one. Our client is a retail coal dealer. The product is domestic coal. An analysis brings out the fact (1) that we are able to offer a worth-while saving, (2) that we are selling good clean quality coal, (3) that it can be bought on a convenient budget basis.

An analysis of the market shows that our prospects are the everyday sort of people, interested in getting the necessities of life at the lowest possible cost. To get the letter off to a good start, let's arouse interest by beginning:

Wouldn't it be a grand and glorious feeling, when the time comes to start the heater fire next Fall, to know that your entire season's coal supply has been paid for—almost without your knowing it—at a real saving!

Certainly that should get them to go on if only to find out what the letter is about. So let's continue to arouse interest by telling them:

Well, that's exactly what the Mathers' Budget Plan enables you to do, and here's how it works:

Those last five words are almost certain to get the reader into the third paragraph, so now we can start stating the proposition:

Anytime between now and June 1st, give us your order for as many tons of good clean Mathers' coal as you think you will need next Winter. You'll save real money, because we will accept your order at the low Spring prices, which go up again, as you know, in the Fall.

Now we must explain how easy it is to save and tell something of the method. So we go on:

Pay as little as $1 per week, depending on the size of your order, throughout the Summer. You'll hardly miss these small weekly payments, and when "heater season" comes again, you'll be all set for Winter, without having to even think about ordering coal—or paying for it! We will make complete delivery before November 1st, or as the coal is paid for, whichever you prefer.

It's time now to start leading up to the "action" part of the letter, so let's ask a question:

Doesn't this sound like a sensible procedure . . . a wise investment? Many of our customers took advantage of the plan last year, and they tell us that buying coal this way is both easy and pleasant.

Finally there is the close—driving for a phone call or a return of the enclosed reply card so that the salesman will have some definite leads to work on:

Call us on the phone, today, or if you prefer to have a representative call, mail the card. Remember, all orders must be placed before June 1st to insure low Spring prices!

Here is the completed letter:

Wouldn't it be a grand and glorious feeling, when the time comes to start the heater fire again, next Fall, to know that your entire season's coal supply had been paid for . . . almost without your knowing it . . . and at a *real saving?*

Well, that's exactly what the Mathers' Budget Plan enables you to do; and here's how it works:

Anytime between now and June 1st, give us your order for as many tons of good, clean Mathers' coal as you think you will need next Winter. *You'll save real money,* because we will accept your order at the *low Spring prices,* which go up again, as you know, in the Fall.

Pay as little as one dollar per week, depending on the size of your order, throughout the Summer. You'll hardly miss these small weekly payments, and when "heater season" comes again, you'll be all set for Winter, without having to even think about ordering coal . . . *or paying for it!* We will make complete delivery before November 1st, or as the coal is paid for, whichever you prefer.

Doesn't this sound like a sensible procedure . . . a *wise investment?* Many of our customers took advantage of the plan last year, and they tell us that buying coal was really both easy and pleasant.

Call us on the phone today, or if you prefer to have a representative call, mail the card. Remember, all orders must be placed before June 1st, to insure *low Spring prices!*

Sincerely,

P.S. When you have paid for three tons or more, and delivery has been made, we will give you a beautiful clock, absolutely free, in appreciation of your business.

Problem No. 2. Our client is a high-grade resort hotel. Its service and facilities constitute the "product." Analysis shows that the things we have to talk about are new low rates, good food, safety of construction, golf and other sports, the exclusiveness of the hotel, etc.

Our prospects are a selected group of people, of the type that would be acceptable to the management and guests and who can afford to pay the price for fine accommodations.

The proposition is a good one because of the recent reduction in rates—in short, we can offer the same advantages but for considerably less money.

We're off. Let's open up by getting in some suggestion of *news,* which always carries them on to the second paragraph:

> You'll be agreeably surprised to learn how inexpensively you can now enjoy a vacation at one of the smartest, most exclusive mountain resorts in the East.

Having started with the subject of cost, we'll naturally have to follow through, but, before we really tell them the news, let's justify the former rates, which were unquestionably high. Then from that statement, we lead them to the lower rates in effect now:

> The rates at Buckwood Inn have always been commensurate with the character of its service, with the excellence of its food, with the unusual facilities for enjoyment.

> Today, although Buckwood Inn has just as much to offer, is just as ideal for a perfect vacation, the rates are very materially lowered, as you will see from the enclosed

folder. We are still catering, of course, to the same carefully selected group of people.

Here would be a good place to inject some effective sales copy about the "product." We pick on "safety" because of the reputation most mountain hotels have for being firetraps:

One interesting point about Buckwood Inn is the solid cement and tile construction that makes it absolutely fireproof. We are free completely from the fire menace associated with the usual country hotel.

A frank suggestion to take advantage of these low rates and the unusual facilities would be in order now, so:

With the three best months in the year ahead of you, why not plan now to come up here in the mountains and enjoy the finest vacation you've ever had...at probably the lowest cost?

Another argument to reach the ones who enjoy golf:

The golf course, one of the most widely known in America, is in excellent condition and the green fees are the lowest in history.

The close, because of the character of the hotel, shouldn't be too strong:

Your reservation or request for further information will receive immediate and interested attention.

Here's the completed letter:

You'll be agreeably surprised to learn how inexpensively you can now enjoy a vacation at one of the smartest, most exclusive mountain resorts in the East.

The rates at Buckwood Inn have always been commensurate with the character of its service, with the excellence of its food, with the unusual facilities for enjoyment.

Today, although Buckwood Inn has just as much to offer, is just as ideal for a perfect vacation, the rates are very materially lowered, as you will see from the enclosed folder. We are still catering, of course, to the same carefully selected group of people.

One interesting point about Buckwood Inn is the solid cement and tile construction that makes it absolutely fireproof. We are free completely from the fire menace associated with the usual country hotel.

With the three best months in the year ahead of you, why not plan now to come up here in the mountains and enjoy the finest vacation you've ever had . . . at probably the lowest cost?

The golf course, one of the most widely known in America, is in excellent condition and the green fees are the lowest in history.

Your reservation or request for further information will receive immediate and interested attention.

Problem No. 3. This case history is about a manufacturer who has just introduced a new type of overall for youngsters. It is unique in that on the pockets there are large cutout pictures, in color, of the well-known and popular characters "Bugs Bunny" and "Elmer." Full-page trade-paper ads have been prepared and are to appear in a forthcoming issue of the business magazines reaching department stores, infants' and children's shops, etc. Our job now is to prepare a letter to the trade, selling them on the idea of ordering this new product on the strength of anticipated quick acceptance by the consuming public.

We're not going to use personal fill-ins on this letter because there are too many company names on the list to make it practical.

Our first job is to get the letter off to a good start, so let's concentrate on a headline that will make the recipient *want* to read the first paragraph. How about this—

SENSATIONAL NEW IDEA
IN CHILDREN'S WEAR!

Don't you agree that many buyers in a department store who read such a headline would *read on* to find out what it was all about?

That's the initial step in our attempt to create *interest* and the first paragraph should continue with the same objective in mind. Like this—

> Talk about enthusiasm! You should have seen the head buyer of one of the largest department stores in the country when she first laid eyes on BUNNYALL—*the overall that grows with the child.*

Having aroused some interest in the product, we now attempt to create *a desire* on the part of the buyer by continuing to build up the market possibilities of the product. As, for instance, with this second paragraph:

> And with good reason, for there's nothing quite like BUNNYALL on the market. There are plenty of overalls, of course, but there are *none* with the DOUBLE appeal you have with this one.

The third paragraph follows through with a further build-up—

> BUNNYALL *makes an instant hit with the kids,* thanks to

Bugs Bunny and Elmer, prominently pictured on the pockets.

The next paragraph helps to build *conviction,* while further selling the market possibilities of the product, by talking about the advertising.

BUNNYALL *makes just as big a hit with mothers,* thanks to exclusive features that you'll find fully described in the attached reprint. This ad will appear in the August issues of *Infant's and Children's Review,* and *Earnshaw's Infant's, Children's and Girl's Wear.*

Now we get down to the question of *action.* This we do by suggesting a possible delay in delivery due to the anticipated popularity of the product. Here are the *action* paragraphs—

Based on the way BUNNYALL has already been received, it is safe to say we'll be swamped with orders very shortly after the announcement ads appear. That's why we are sending you this advance notice. We believe you will want to get the jump on your competitors by stocking BUNNYALL *now.*

Orders will, of course, be filled in accordance with the way they are received, so please don't put it off. Mail your orders *today.*

Here is the finished letter—

SENSATIONAL NEW IDEA
IN CHILDREN'S WEAR!

Talk about enthusiasm! You should have seen the head buyer of one of the largest department stores in the country when she first laid eyes on BUNNYALL—*the overall that grows with the child.*

And with good reason, for there's nothing quite like

BUNNYALL on the market. There are plenty of overalls, of course, but there are *none* with the DOUBLE appeal you have with this one.

BUNNYALL *makes an instant hit with the kids,* thanks to Bugs Bunny and Elmer, prominently pictured on the pockets.

BUNNYALL *makes just as big a hit with the mothers,* thanks to exclusive features that you'll find fully described in the attached reprint. This ad will appear in the August issues of *Infant's and Children's Review,* and *Earnshaw's Infant's, Children's and Girl's Wear.*

Based on the way BUNNYALL has already been received, it is safe to say we'll be swamped with orders very shortly after these announcement ads appear. That's why we are sending you this advance notice. We believe you will want to get the jump on your competitors by stocking BUNNYALL now.

Orders will, of course, be filled in accordance with the way they are received, so please don't put it off. Mail yours *today.*

Problem No. 4. Our client is a distributor and refiner of lubricating oil, the kind used in automotive and Diesel engines. This particular letter is about an oil that was originally developed for Diesel but is just as effective in automotive engines, and we are attempting to sell that idea to new car dealers. The feature of the oil is that it can withstand the higher working temperatures and pressures of the modern engine and that, unlike other oils, it does not break down under these conditions and increase friction, deposit sludge, produce varnish, etc., etc. The letter is accompanied by a single-page 8½ by 11 circular which gives *proof* of efficiency. Since it is very obviously a circular letter, let's not go to the expense of a personal fill-in but use a three-line heading instead:

> We developed it for Diesels
> *—here's proof that it's perfect*
> *also for gasoline engines!*

With that as a starter, let's open up by saying:

> If you're interested in superior performance for cars and trucks—and we mean really superior—you'll welcome this news with open arms.

Now we should start to build up the story, telling what we have accomplished with Diesel lubricating oil. We have to establish that as being successful before switching over to the main story:

> For years, we have been perfecting Bannerlube Diesel lubricating oil. It is being used successfully now all over the east and has conclusively demonstrated its ability to do a better lubricating job under the hardest possible conditions—*in a full compression engine.*

Here's where we swing over to the oil for gasoline engines, which is where the new car dealer comes in:

> We figured that if it would do that, it would be a "walkaway" in a gasoline engine which just has a high compression head. It was!

Next step is to start building conviction, which we do by offering proof:

> After many tests and comparisons, the most recent of which is related on the attached sheet "Proof of the Pudding," we are ready to furnish you with what one new car dealer says is "by far the most satisfactory oil we have used."

Now we start the selling job on the automotive oil:

Here is a modern oil—made expressly for modern engines which, due to high power output and small clearances, definitely require a lubricating oil that can withstand the higher working temperatures and pressures. Old-style oils break down under these conditions and increase friction, deposit sludge, produce varnish—which in turn sticks rings and valves, causes pistons to drag and reduces engine power and gasoline mileage.

Finally, we try to arouse interest in the attached folder which gives more complete information about these products, and at the same time make our bid for action:

You'll find the story of Bannerlube and the advantages of OILIER LUBRICATION in the enclosed folder. Won't you read it carefully and then let us come in and, without obligation, give you our recommendation—in terms of your own needs?

Thus we have another letter finished:

> ### We developed it for Diesels
> *—here's proof that it's perfect*
> *also for gasoline engines!*

If you're interested in superior performance for cars and trucks—*and we mean really superior*—you'll welcome this news with open arms.

For years, we have been perfecting Bannerlube Diesel lubricating oil. It is being used successfully now all over the east and has conclusively demonstrated its ability to do a better lubricating job under the hardest possible conditions—in a full compression engine.

We figured that if it would do that, it would be a

"walkaway" in a gasoline engine which just has a high compression head. It was!

After many tests and comparisons, the most recent of which is related on the attached sheet "Proof of the Pudding," we are ready to furnish you with what one new car dealer says is "by far the most satisfactory oil we have used."

Here is modern oil—made expressly for modern engines which, due to high power output and small clearances, definitely require a lubricating oil that can withstand the higher working temperatures and pressures. Old-style oils break down under these conditions and increase friction, deposit sludge, produce varnish—which in turn sticks rings and valves, causes pistons to drag and reduces engine power and gasoline mileage.

You'll find the story of Bannerlube and the advantages of OILIER LUBRICATION in the enclosed folder. Won't you read it carefully and then let us come in, and without obligation, give you our recommendation—in terms of your own needs?

Problem No. 5. A manufacturer of furnace cement wants to reach the stove manufacturers who buy cement, not only for their own use but to include with every order for a stove. The facts are these: This cement we are to sell will give more coverage, will stand more heat, has more flexibility, and will not harden in the package as many of the others on the market do. On top of all that, we can offer an extra discount to induce them to buy.

The prospects are buying another brand of furnace cement now and are apparently satisfied. Our only hope is to sell them on the idea that by buying ours they'll be getting a better product for a lower cost. That would seem to be a pretty good proposition.

We might open this attack by asking a point-blank, interest-arousing question:

> Are you open for an unusually good "buy" in furnace cement?

Let's further the interest in the savings we're holding out before the reader by saying:

> We are looking for firms who are willing to use a finer product in order to enjoy a substantial saving. Believe it or not, such firms will be getting the "cake and the penny" both!

We'd better prove it now by bringing in a few facts to build conviction:

> They can buy with every assurance that I.B.M. Asbestos Furnace Cement will give one-fifth more coverage than any similar product they have ever used; that it will stand more heat than iron and retain positive bond to iron at extreme temperatures; that it possesses unusual flexibility after setting; and that it won't harden in the package.

There are two parts to this argument, one stressing the "finer product" and the other—well, let's put it down:

> Now for the SAVINGS. Note the low list prices on the enclosed postcard. From these you are entitled to the full jobber's discount, 50–5–30%.
>
> But as a special inducement to order now, we will, for a limited time, allow an EXTRA TEN PER CENT! Furthermore, if you'd like to try out I.B.M. Asbestos Furnace Cement first, we'll send you a 3-pound sample free. Could anything be fairer?

We've supplied a real inducement to buy and proved to the prospect that he can feel perfectly comfortable about the quality. All we should need now is something to turn the interest we have aroused into some kind of action. How about a question like this:

Wouldn't it pay you to mail off the card today?

Put all these thoughts together and we have our letter:

Are you open for an unusually good "buy" in furnace cement?

We are looking for firms who are willing to use a finer product in order to enjoy a substantial saving. Believe it or not, such firms will be getting the "cake and the penny" both!

They can buy with every assurance that I.B.M. Asbestos Furnace Cement will give one-fifth more coverage than any similar product they have ever used; that it will stand more heat than iron and retain positive bond to iron at extreme temperatures; that it possesses unusual flexibility after setting; and that it won't harden in the package.

Now for the savings. Note the low list prices on the enclosed postcard. From these you are entitled to the full jobber's discount, 50–5–30%.

But as a special inducement to order now, we will, for a limited time, allow an extra ten per cent! Furthermore, if you'd like to try out I.B.M. Asbestos Furnace Cement first, we'll send you a 3-pound sample free. Could anything be fairer?

Wouldn't it pay you to mail off the card today?

CHAPTER EIGHT *Pointers on Letters to Different Kinds of Prospects*

Letters to Executives

The word "executive" covers a lot of ground, because there are as many different kinds as there are different kinds of human beings. There are certain characteristics, however, that place an executive in a somewhat different prospect category from a professional man, for instance, or a homeowner, even though he may be also an executive. It is strange that you should have to write differently to men at home and the same men at their offices, but you do. The reason, of course, is that at home there are leisure and quiet. A man has time to read and is frequently glad to read anything that looks interesting enough or important enough to command attention.

At the office—well, that's a completely different story. Here, your letter, lying in a pile on the desk as your prospect starts through the morning mail, is faced with the stiffest kind of competition for attention. The main thing to keep in mind is: Say what you want to say as briefly as you can and still do justice to it, then stop. Most busy men resent having their time (which they consider valuable, if no one else does) needlessly wasted. Letters to this classification should, generally speaking, be on the "short" side. Granted that any letter, nc matter what its subject or to what kind of prospect it is being sent, should be only *as long as is necessary to tell the story effectively*. Notice I said, "generally speaking." There will be exceptions to this, as to all other rules.

Here is a good letter to executives:

> *Here's an expert for your staff*
> —but NOT for your payroll!

He's the Vanderherchen representative who will welcome the opportunity to check the canvas and canvas products you are now using. Objective—to help you make *sure* you're getting the kind of protective covering that increases the life of your machinery and equipment, or the kind of VAN Bags that save time and money in shipping, storing merchandise, collecting waste, holding work in process.

Too often there is a tendency to re-order "more of the same," when actually a different kind of canvas would give better, longer and cheaper protection, or perhaps a different style VAN Bag would save you additional time and money.

In recent years, there have been a number of new developments in protective coverings. For instance, there are various types of treated canvas that have outmoded plain canvas for specific jobs. New synthetics cannot be equaled for others.

Vanderherchen has kept abreast of all new developments in materials to give you the one best suited to your purpose. Our 50 years' experience in designing bags, coverings, tarpaulins, etc., has given us the solution to practically every kind of canvas problem.

So why not call in a Vanderherchen representative the

next time you need *anything* of canvas. Just drop us a note, or phone RA 5-4197.

Letters to Dealers

By dealers, I mean the medium-size and smaller retail merchants. The heads of large metropolitan stores are really executives and should be treated accordingly. Small dealers, for the most part, are just plain folks. Pumping your letter full of highbrow English won't help you one bit. If you want to convince them that it is to their advantage to accept your proposition, you'll have to use simple language, simply expressed. That is the secret of successful letter writing to dealers. Your letters should be informal, sincere, *natural*— not patronizing in any sense of the word.

Your letters should not only be couched in the dealer's language but written with his problems in mind. Anticipate his reaction to your proposition, and answer his objections before they have a chance to formulate.

Don't set him up as an "easy mark" just because he lives in a small town or has a small store in the city. Give him credit for good sense, whether he actually has any or not.

Be interesting in any event, helpful if possible, but never "preachy."

All dealers are interested, primarily, in profit, turnover, repeat business, time saving, money saving, improved conditions, and the like, not in facts about your product, except as they may be turned in some way into benefits or advantages to them.

The following letter to dealers keeps these things in mind. It's one of a regular monthly series:

WHAT'S THE SECRET
IN SELLING PIANOS?

To put the question another way, what magic formula can a dealer use to get the absolute maximum in piano sales out of his territory?

Shall we tell you?

THERE AIN'T NO SUCH ANIMAL!

But don't misunderstand, *there is a way* to get every ounce of piano business out of your area no matter where you live, but there's no secret or magic formula about it. It just means taking advantage of every opportunity to get prospects into your store.

The most successful piano dealers, the ones making the most profit, literally don't miss a trick—

> They use regular display advertising in the newspapers
>
> They use classified ads, too
>
> They use the radio
>
> They use television spots
>
> They use direct mail with telephone follow-ups
>
> They put to use all the sales aids they receive from the Lester factory—like, for instance, our new movie, "Keys to Happiness."

The thing we try to keep in mind is that our competition isn't just the other piano companies—it's everybody who is making a bid for the consumer dollar. Automobiles, air-conditioners, radios, television sets—they're all trying to get the money we'd like people to spend for pianos.

That's why we keep urging you to advertise *consistently*—in as many ways as you can afford. Believe me, and we know from experience—IT PAYS!

Letters to Jobbers

Much of the story on dealers applies to jobbers, even though they are usually larger operators. Jobbers, or wholesalers, are not so much interested in the consumer angle of your proposition, except indirectly as their interests are affected by public demand or acceptance. They are more familiar with and interested in economic conditions, the trend of buying conditions, etc., than is the small retailer. They have hundreds and frequently thousands of items on their lists, and therefore the attention that can be devoted to any one is necessarily limited. The motive used to get a jobber to push one particular item in his line must be unusually strong if the letter is to accomplish its purpose.

Here's a good letter to jobbers which also contains a good idea:

> We are gathering together, right now, some extremely helpful information about roof coatings, furnace cement, plastic cement and similar products that should help every jobber's salesman increase his volume.
>
> May we send it to you and to your men each month as it comes out?
>
> There is naturally a lot about coatings and cements that the average salesman couldn't be expected to know. To many of them one roof coating, for instance, is like any other—whereas actually there is a tremendous difference. The facts that we plan to present in these monthly Bulletins will enable your men to demonstrate that beyond the slightest doubt. We expect also to include from time to time money-making ideas for retailers . . . ideas that your men can use to decided advantage.
>
> By the time our lists are complete, the first batch of

facts will be ready to go out. Won't you, therefore, fill out the attached sheet promptly and put it in the mail back to us? We'll appreciate your cooperation.

Letters to Schools, Colleges, Etc.

No matter how much you break down the population into groups, they're still *people,* human beings with different likes and dislikes, different ambitions and problems, but nevertheless with many similarities. They are alike in *this* respect, for instance: They all respond more readily if approached by means of the letter formula.

In writing to schools and colleges, as in writing to any other specific group, be sure you start by arousing interest, follow up by creating desire, then build conviction by stating facts, giving proof where possible, then go after some kind of action. Remember, too, that the names of schools and colleges are easy to get. They therefore receive a lot of mail, and because of that it is imperative that your letter contain a "stopper" in the first paragraph—something that will insure further reading—and then get right down to the business of *selling*.

Notice how both requirements are met in the following letter:

Would you mind a personal question? The answer is really none of our business, but is extremely important to you. Is your present refrigeration system entirely SAFE? And do you KNOW that it is?

If you are using old and obsolete equipment, you will, we feel sure, be interested in this announcement of the only perfected air conditioned refrigeration system on the market—Standard's patented, streamlined UTILITY REFRIGERATOR.

With such a box, all fear of the consequences of a

breakdown would be eliminated for many years to come. Your refrigeration system would be not only safe, but the most efficient yet devised. Repairs, replacements and all of the many problems that are the constant companion of a worn-out refrigerator would be solved as by magic. And, more important, you would be able to keep, in perfect condition, a greater quantity of food, in less space and for a longer period of time.

If you will return the enclosed request-for-information card, we shall be glad to show you how you can install a new Standard Conditioned-Air System, have all the advantages of perfect refrigeration and at the same time SAVE MONEY. Send off the card today while it's right before you.

Letters to Investors

Cautious people, these. Their names appear on the list because they are supposed to have money. And most folks with money are loath to toss it away without at least putting up a struggle. Your letters to this group should have, above all else, *believability*. The tendency is to take what you say with a "grain of salt" anyway. Even before the letter is started, the reader is on the defensive. You must keep this fact always in mind when attempting to sell anything to a list of so-called investors. Be as disarming as you possibly can. Be sincere. Be convincing. See if you don't agree that this letter, a follow-up used to sell subscriptions to a weekly market bulletin, has the proper qualifications.

Suppose you had taken a trial subscription to TREND-OMETER MARKET BULLETINS at the time we wrote you about them, a few weeks ago.

A copy of one of the bulletins you would have received

is enclosed, dated January 21st. Would you mind reading it now, in the light of what has actually happened to the Stocks and Commodities mentioned? You'll find it startlingly accurate.

Isn't it possible, if you'd had this TRENDOMETER BULLETIN and had followed its advice, that you might have saved many times the cost of a TRENDOMETER subscription for an entire year?

One thing you'll like about TRENDOMETER BULLETINS is the ease with which you can read them. No "wading through" is necessary. They're all "meat"—solid, substantial information with the trimmings left off.

You can read them in three minutes, grasp the message instantly, yet despite their briefness, following their advice might easily mean thousands of dollars to you in savings or increased revenue.

TRENDOMETER BULLETINS are written in such a way as to give the busy executive important and essential information about the TREND of the market, quickly and concisely.

I feel confident that after you have received them, even for a few weeks, you will benefit sufficiently to want to keep on receiving them indefinitely.

That's why I am glad to accept a trial subscription. I *know* that TRENDOMETER BULLETINS *will sell themselves,* if given the opportunity.

Why not let me send them to you for a few weeks, so that you can see how "different," how completely understandable and helpful they are. Then, if you decide that you want them to keep coming, as I feel confident you will, the $3.00 you have spent can apply on the subscription price for six months or a year.

If your trial subscription comes in promptly, we will

still include, without extra charge, the personal comments on the stocks you now own, provided they are included in the 200 issues which we regularly study.

This extra service is well worth having, so put your
subscription in the mail today. No money need accompany your order.

Letters to Undertakers

This type of prospect is in business for the same reason that
all other businessmen are—to make a satisfactory living.
Hence he should be talked to in much the same vein, *i.e.,* in
terms of new business, success, profit. Following is a letter
used by a retail floor-covering establishment to sell under-
takers the idea of new rugs and carpets.

May we show you how important floor coverings are to
the success of your business?

Actually, you have only service to sell. It is the degree
of smoothness, of nicety, with which you perform your
delicate task that sends people to you for assistance in
their bereavement.

The proper selection of rugs or carpets can give your
establishment the atmosphere it should have—one of
restfulness, comfort and quiet beauty.

Wear is an important factor, too, for if proper floor
coverings will attract business, it is essential that constant
use does not destroy the value of the investment.

Yes, floor coverings can very easily pay for themselves—in goodwill and new business—but they must be
the right kind.

Our new selection of Hardwick & Magee Company patterns and colorings is now complete. You can see them
here, or if you prefer, call (telephone number) and we
shall be glad to send an especially trained man to see you.

Letters to College Alumni

Don't ever get the idea that *these* are easy letters to write. A man is, we'll say, five years out of college. He dropped out of his Alumni Association two or three years ago for any one of a variety of reasons, has been written to numerous times since. How can you write to him now in such a way as to get a check for renewal of membership? That's the problem, and, in my opinion, there is only one way to solve it. Revive the *spirit of school loyalty that is so strong in the heart of every student and that never completely dies.* And use not one letter, but many—all hammering away on the same heartstring. Here is the second in a series used by the General Alumni Society of the University of Pennsylvania:

> "In days of old as we are told
> There lived a man named Ben;
> A friend was he and *so are we*
> To Pennsylvania Men."

Remember that verse in our song to Ben Franklin? I like it because it seems to express the spirit of friendship and goodwill that exists throughout the entire Alumni Society. To me it's inspiring to think of Pennsylvania graduates all together, as one big, friendly family, with ties so strong they just can't be broken.

To me it's wonderful to keep alive the memory of the happiest years of our lives, to keep informed on what's going on around the old campus, to get first hand and accurate information on the University's Bicentennial, Founder's Day, Election of Alumni Trustees and other important events.

These are just a few of the many reasons why membership in the General Alumni Society has meant so much to me. They are the same reasons why I know you are going to keep *your* membership.

Your annual dues became payable on the first of this month. So that the Society can continue the grand work it's doing, won't you put your check in the mail promptly?

I am asking you personally, not just because the Society urgently needs the loyal support of every Alumnus, but because I'm sure you won't want to be out of touch with the many important activities of your own University, even for a single month.

Letters to Advertising Agencies

Being the head of one, this should be easy. Unfortunately, however, the fact only serves to highlight the obstacles to be surmounted. Advertising men are naturally supercritical when it comes to letters and other advertising material aimed in their direction. The tendency is to look on each letter, mailing piece, or advertisement as a *specimen,* as the brain child of a competitor, as the embodiment of an idea, as a thought stimulator for some project of their own. In writing to advertising men, therefore, keep that in mind. Accept the challenge and make them, in spite of themselves, read your message for the interest it contains. Following closely the letter formula will help achieve that result. Here is an example:

The design of a product plays such an important part in the sales picture these days that I feel sure you will be interested in reading, and keeping the enclosed booklet.

To many of your clients, this will be a year of competitive selling. The advertising you prepare for them will have a tougher job to do, unless some new talking points can be created in the product itself. It is quite possible that you will want to recommend to such clients a radical change in the design of their products, their containers, or both.

The booklet tells about Industrial Design in terms of increased sales. It tells how "Beautility" can be injected into a product to give it more appeal for the buyer, made not only better looking, but better performing and more readily acceptable to more people.

It also tells—we might as well admit it—about Van Sciver Associates, a group of seasoned, scientifically trained specialists in Industrial Design. Be that as it may, we have deliberately put into the booklet information that we feel confident you will find interesting and profitable.

A preliminary discussion about the products of any of your clients might easily prove advantageous to all concerned. May we at least talk about it sometime?

Letters to the Medical and Dental Professions

It is a good idea in writing to these classes not to have your letter smack too much of advertising. Keep it on a dignified basis. Not stiff and formal, but not too informal either. Granted, doctors and dentists are human beings like all the rest of us and react to the same emotions. There are cases where you can afford to be almost facetious in talking to them. But, generally speaking, your letter will be more successful if it avoids extravagant claims, high-pressure salesmanship, and anything bordering on familiarity.

Here is a good letter to doctors:

Dear Doctor—

Which one of these four BONUS BOOKS would you like

to have without cost or obligation? Name it ... and the
Editors of J. B. Lippincott will send it to you with their
compliments ...

1. *Fluid and Electrolyte Therapy,* by Drs. Franklin
   L. Ashley and Horace G. Love
2. *Stress Situations,* edited by Dr. Samuel Liebman
3. *Low Back Pain and Sciatica,* by Dr. Louis T. Pa-
   lumbo
4. *Regional Enteritis,* by Dr. Frederick F. Boyce

*Any one of these fact-filled books will be included, for
a very limited time, in a new subscription to the American Practitioner and Digest of Treatment—at no extra
charge!*

TAKE ADVANTAGE OF THIS OPPORTUNITY TO RECEIVE
A $3 BOOK FREE BY SUBSCRIBING TODAY!

Subscribe to American Practitioner and Digest of
Treatment—get to know this unusual medical magazine
—and you'll wonder how you ever got along without it!

For one thing—it will enable you to cut your required
reading time in HALF!

For another—it will bring you, month after month,
up-to-date information prepared by physicians, clinicians,
specialists who know your needs and problems, and who
are well aware that with every busy, practicing physician,
time for reading is hard to find.

Think of the practical value of a publication which
brings you authentic and helpful material on new tech-
nics, applications, procedures and drugs ... first hand
original reports on late clinical developments ... reports
on medical meetings you haven't time to attend ... case
histories from the wards of the Massachusetts General
Hospital.

Think of the time *this* single feature saves you—

DIGESTS OF FROM 25 TO 40 ARTICLES CULLED FROM
AT LEAST 150 LEADING PROFESSIONAL PERIODICALS
—THE "MEAT" IN THE AUTHOR'S OWN WORDS

Thousands of busy practitioners have found—as you will, too—that the easiest, quickest way to keep up with medical progress is by regular reading of American Practitioner and Digest of Treatment.

It would be profitable, under any circumstances, to subscribe now because of this unusual opportunity to get FREE any one of the $3 books listed on page 1 of this letter.

Keep in mind that you take no risk, for you may cancel your subscription to American Practitioner and Digest of Treatment anytime after the second issue. And if you should decide to do that, *you may keep the bonus book.*

I hope you will take advantage of this special get-acquainted offer quickly, for it must be withdrawn when our limited supply of the books is gone. *Be sure to get the copy you want . . . mail the enclosed card TODAY.* Just sign and mail—we pay the postage.

And here is another:

Dear Doctor:

Here is a brand new book on SEX . . . by a Physician for Physicians' use, and we think one of the most valuable contributions made so far to this tremendously important subject.

SEXUAL HYGIENE AND PATHOLOGY—By John F. Oliven, M.D.

In this manual, written on a professional level through-out, all aspects of sexuality are described with a clinical frankness which sets it apart from other books on sex.

In it, you'll find many areas of special interest to you in your day-to-day work, much sound, practical material to help you handle the sexual problems of your patients:

> —how to instruct parents who have difficulties with their children's sex education; the technic of pre-marital examination and instruction; varying approaches to frigidity in women; sexual advice in heart disease, obesity and other special situations—to mention just a few.

Here is the latest knowledge of human sexuality, normal and abnormal, knowledge which every doctor can use with profit in his practice. The manual reviews all known normal aspects of sexuality, gives full descriptions and directions concerning sex-hygienic situations and problems, covers all sexual distress states which you are likely to encounter.

NONE APPROACHES OLIVEN'S MANUAL FOR COMPREHENSIVENESS

In this manual, everything, theory or practice, has been reexamined in the light of modern clinical experience, either the author's own, or the best available findings in this country and elsewhere. It must be remembered that some concepts in vogue as few as 20 years ago have been superseded or discredited today.

Sexual Hygiene and Pathology is organized in four parts . . . Sexuality in Childhood . . . Sexuality in the Second Decade—Sexuality of the Normal Adult—Sexual Pathology. All phases and factors are discussed—social, endocrine, psychologic, medical and others. All aspects incorporated—from postcoital douching to management of the married homosexual—from the current trend of sex instruction on the High School level to the course and prognosis of sexual recrudescences in elderly men. This book is COMPLETE! It literally covers all phases of sex counseling and for that section alone is well worth the cost.

Let me emphasize, Doctor, that this is a *manual for the physician* (*that,* in fact, is its sub-title) available only through registered medical bookstores or direct from Lippincott. It is in no sense a book for laymen. It is in *every* sense a compendium of modern sexual knowledge for the practicing physician.

Won't you make use of Lippincott's offer of 10-day Free examination? Send the enclosed form today. No obligation, of course.

Letters to Architects

These prospects are also professional men, but of a somewhat different type. It is extremely important to know something about the architect's business, his specialized relations with clients, manufacturers, contractors, etc. Letters to this group should be as personal-looking as possible. Hoovenizing or a similar electric-typewriter process is a good investment. The next best thing, since individually typewritten letters are impractical for a large list, is a good, clean, multigraphed letter with a fill-in that really matches.

Architects want facts. They'll "eat up" all the useful or helpful information you can give them. And they'll throw away all the purely self-centered letters they can get their hands on.

The following letter to architects "got across":

> Now! Tough, durable flooring for
> new buildings . . . or how to make an
> *old* floor *new* again!

The perfect flooring for factories, hospitals, shops, warehouses—in fact, any place where floor traffic is heavy or hard—that's SELBALITH!

The enclosed folder gives you all the details on SELBA-LITH, including specifications and application information. Look it over—see for yourself the many advantages of SELBALITH as a floor covering. You'll note the extreme *versatility* of SELBALITH: It can be used as original flooring; to resurface old or badly worn flooring—asphalt tile, rubber tile, linoleum, etc. It is long-wearing . . . tough . . . durable. Truly an ideal flooring for every building need. Even if you are not now in the market for either new or replacement flooring, you'll find the information in this folder well worth holding for future reference.

And don't forget, Selby, Battersby & Company can also *install* SELBALITH for you. Our experienced applicators complete the team needed to give you a superior floor for all your traffic needs: *the right mix and a contractor who knows his business.*

We'll be glad to quote on any sized flooring or re-flooring need without obligation. For further information or specific quotations, fill out and mail the enclosed card today.

Here is another, following the same rules, but of a different type:

With the cost of materials and labor what they are these days, you must often find yourself hard put to give clients the effects they want and still keep estimates from getting out of hand. That's why I think you'll be interested in hearing some facts about the new, improved Parkay.

This beautiful, solid Appalachian oak floor and wall

covering offers unlimited possibilities for creating luxurious interiors at a surprisingly low cost. Parkay combines all the rich, natural beauty, the unusual durability of gleaming polished hardwood, with the structural advantages of modern custom-built flooring.

Parkay is available in tiles or random-width planks—comes completely prefinished even to waxing and polishing—with its magnificent cabinet finish permanently preserved by a special scratch-resistant finish. It is extremely simple to install; an average room can be floored or paneled with Parkay in a matter of hours. And once installed, Parkay is so easy to maintain that upkeep is reduced to a minimum.

You'll want to see the new Parkay for yourself and study its advantages at your leisure. If you will simply return the enclosed card, we'll see that you receive a sample and complete information—without the slightest obligation, of course.

Letters to Women

Don't think for a minute that you can write to women in the same vein as to men. They represent a completely different kind of human being. If you have any business dealings with them, it will pay you to do a little serious "studying up" on the subject.

One thing that makes it difficult is that there are so *many* different varieties. Far be it from me to attempt to outline them, because in the first place I couldn't if I wanted to and in the second place it wouldn't do any good if I could. What particular kind of woman buys your particular product—well, that's your problem, not mine. I can, however, point out a few general characteristics, good to keep in mind.

Women are more appreciative of beauty than men. Style,

of course, means more to them. The appearance of anything—an automobile, home, piece of furniture, etc., will loom larger in the woman's mind than in her husband's. Women are frequently shrewd buyers. They influence the purchase of 75 per cent or more of all the goods that are bought. They like details and a lot of information; therefore they will read longer letters, as a rule, than men. They are infinitely more observant; therefore they are quick to see untidiness or poor processing. They are great daydreamers; therefore an interestingly developed word picture will frequently get across with women when a man mightn't take the time to read it. Here's a letter to women that does a complete selling job with the "audience" well in mind.

Dear Friend:

I have some wonderful news for you!

There's a quick, easy way to learn how to sew just like the professionals do—to make, mend and alter clothes for yourself and children, to make slipcovers, curtains and other home furnishings—in short, *to beat the high cost of living and have fun doing it.*

I have just secured for our customers a limited number of one of the most amazing books you ever read—"SEWING FOR EVERYONE," by the nationally famous Mary Brooks Picken.

This is probably the simplest, easiest to understand, most authoritative book on home sewing ever written. It's just filled with "how to do it" illustrations, with A B C directions for beginners and advanced instruction for experts, with short cuts and helpful hints.

You'll be the envy of all your friends and neighbors when they see you in new, smart clothes, perfectly tailored. They'll never guess that you made them yourself, at a fraction of their apparent value.

Haven't you often wished for a new and original idea for a dress, a suit or coat—one with distinctive details and smart lines, styled especially for you? Or for expert advice on adjusting patterns to get a perfect fit so your clothes will have that Tailor-made look? Or for a quick way of making over, smartly, clothes that have become too small, too large or out of date? If you have, then "SEWING FOR EVERYONE" is exactly what you need. For while many women can sew, few women know the "tricks of the trade" and can sew like the professionals do. *But you can,* with the help of this unusual book, even if you've never sewed a stitch before.

You'll learn quickly how to make all the different kinds of clothes that constitute a complete wardrobe—all types of dresses, tailored coats, negligées, housecoats, slips, etc. You'll find step-by-step instruction for all details from start to finish.

You'll learn how to make play suits and dresses for the children that cost practically nothing; how to make over old things, change necklines, remake and refit torn sleeves; how to make tailored pockets, buttonholes, how to use appliqué, shirring, ruffles, bows, picoting, cording, braiding, smocking.

And that isn't all

With the help of this book you can dress up your home too. New slipcovers, curtains, valances, bedspreads, dressing table skirts, mattress covers, etc., are *nothing* to make when you know how. "SEWING FOR EVERYONE" *tells* you how, with so many pictures and diagrams and construction details that a young girl in her teens could follow it with ease. *And many have!*

Think of the thrill you'll have when you demon-

strate to your family and friends what an expert seamstress you have become. Best of all, think of the money you'll save—and remember—it's smart to be thrifty.

Hundreds of women call "SEWING FOR EVERYONE" the best investment they ever made, the household book that brought them the greatest amount of pleasure and profit. And no wonder, for I doubt if there is a single owner of this book who hasn't saved many, many times its slight cost.

EXAMINE IT FOR A WHOLE WEEK *FREE*

Once you see this complete guide to profitable sewing, you'll say to yourself: "This book could easily be worth ten dollars to me." But I'm not going to ask you to pay ten dollars, or eight, or even five. No, as I said at the beginning of this letter, I secured a quantity of these books as a service to our customers because I felt sure you would want one. If I'm right, you can have a copy for only $2.65, providing you act promptly. But I must ask you to put your request for a trial copy *in the return mail.* There will be no obligation to keep it, if after seven days you don't agree it's a most fascinating and useful book, and *worth many times the special price I ask.*

SEND NO MONEY. But fill in and mail the enclosed trial order TODAY to be sure of your copy.

Sincerely,

P.S. SPECIAL GIFT

If you care to send cash with order and mail it promptly, we'll include FREE a copy of "THE MODERN COOK BOOK," filled with recipes and essential cooking information. *And our guarantee still stands.* Your money back if not satisfied.

Letters to Mail-order Buyers

Perhaps we should widen this classification to include all letters that are sent out to get orders as opposed to those whose mission it is to bring back inquiries or those which are not expected to bring back anything at all (as letters that simply pave the way for a salesman). A letter whose job it is to get a prospect actually to commit himself either to an order on approval or to an advance payment in cash must obviously do a selling job from start to finish.

It can leave no questions unanswered, no doubts in the prospect's mind about the product, as to what it does, what it has done, how it works, what it looks like, who has used it or bought it, why it's better, why it's a good value, and what it costs.

Be complete in your description but be interesting while you're doing it. The very fact that you have to cover so much ground usually necessitates a long letter; the longer it is, the more care must be taken in carrying the reader logically through from one paragraph to the next. Much more necessary in this than in any other type of letter is the letter formula—*interest, desire, conviction,* and *action.* The letter must have interest or its two, three, or four pages of closely typewritten copy will not be read; it must create desire or you might as well be talking to a stone wall; it must carry conviction or the desire you've created will be left in mid-air; and it must cause action to be taken or you'll never obtain results from your efforts.

And even that isn't enough. There are certain basic principles of mail selling that *must* be adhered to if you are to enjoy maximum returns. As a matter of fact, there are eight of them, and here they are:

1. Have a product that is in demand by the type of people

to whom the advertising is being mailed—and on which there's both a low delivery cost and a high mark-up to allow a decent profit with what are considered good mail-order returns.

2. Have the most attractive proposition possible—with regard to the product itself, the price and the selling plan (open account, free trial, approval, cash with order, etc.).

3. Have your advertising material (including the envelope) so appealing at first glance that those receiving it will *want* to read it.

4. Have the story told so truthfully, so sincerely, and so convincingly that those reading it will want to possess the product or enjoy the benefits of the service.

5. Include an unqualified *guaranty* that your product or service will do all that is claimed for it.

6. Have a list that contains as nearly 100 per cent live prospects as it is possible to find.

7. Have all mailings tested before being sent to a large list, and then, if sent to a large list later, properly timed so as to be received on the most favorable day.

8. Have or build up such a reputation for fair dealing and good value that the reader of your message will have confidence in your firm.

Here's a good follow-up mail-order letter. Notice the letter formula all through it.

Are you waiting for
something

—before subscribing to the Medlock 12-lesson course in home farming?

Please don't—for your own sake. Be ready by that time to get the very utmost out of your farm, in food, profit, pleasure and security.

Make it self-sufficient. Make yourself independent of business conditions whatever they may be. Learn now how to run that farm of yours so that IT PAYS!

I feel confident you'll find this course a veritable encyclopedia of home farming, yet easy to learn, easy to understand and follow, because it is *based on successful experience*. From every single lesson I'll guarantee you'll learn something that will enable you to get better results.

The *very first lesson* can save you money, for it tells how to choose, stock and work the farm, profitably. It is chock-full of practical, useful information that will spark your enthusiasm at once. Also there's a valuable appendix on necessary tools and machinery.

You'll learn how to plan production in *Lesson No. 2,* and this is one of the vital requirements of successful home farming. It answers your questions on how much to produce, how much to plant, how many animals are needed and a host of other questions. Please remember, each subject or question is answered in *full detail*.

Every good farm has a garden. In *Lesson No. 3,* you'll read all about gardens—what and how to plant; what vegetables to grow for storing or preserving; feed crops and other necessary information.

In *Lessons 4 through 8,* you'll get a complete library of facts on farm animals. *No. 4* covers all the dairy operations; *No. 5* tells about poultry; *No. 6* will make you like pigs, as well as tell you how to raise them profitably; *No. 7* discusses sheep and wool, goats, rabbits, dogs, wild fur-bearing animals, pets, etc.; *No. 8* talks dollars and *sense* about meat production on the home farm.

Canning and preserving of fruits, vegetables and meats is detailed in *Lesson No. 9* with money-saving tips on methods, storing, etc. We even cover rat-proofing in this complete lesson.

Lesson No. 10 answers your questions about orchards —tells about planning, planting, cultivation, trimming, spraying, grafting and harvesting.

Your woodlot is covered in *Lesson No. 11,* and you'll be amazed at the treasure-trove of valuable information here.

The successful home farm should yield a surplus. So *Lesson No. 12* will tell you how to dispose of it both at wholesale and retail, will also give you a simple, practical accounting system to use in keeping a record of results. Dyeing and weaving, spinning, garment-making, metal and wood working, pottery, leather, trades and specialties are grouped under Cottage Industries in this final chapter.

The important thing to remember is that IF YOU ONLY GET ONE GOOD IDEA OUT OF THIS COURSE, at its present low price, it could easily be a fine investment. The fact is, you'll get dozens of practical ideas and a great deal of dependable information on *how* and *when* to do everything.

Remember, you not only receive the regular 12-lesson course, but also the Medlock Farm Diary, issued once a month to subscribers at no extra cost. Here you'll find helpful hints and short cuts that will prove of inestimable value to you throughout the entire year.

Remember also the one year consultation service that is available to you without extra charge if your enrollment comes in promptly.

Since there's so much chance for gain and so little for loss (complete satisfaction guaranteed or your money refunded at any time during the course), why not send off your enrollment form *today* and get started?

Here is another mail selling letter. Read it carefully with the letter formula in mind. You'll see INTEREST—DESIRE—CONVICTION—ACTION almost as plainly as if they were written in the margin.

Read how your SPEAKING VOICE
can easily be turned into
your most profitable asset

> Do you want to improve your business and social status? Would you like to develop more poise and personality? Do you want to attain the highest possible "dollars and cents" kind of success?

Then let me tell you how *your voice* can become your most powerful asset rather than a hindering liability.

YOUR VOICE REFLECTS YOUR PERSONALITY. From your first "good morning" to your last "good night" you affect others by the way you speak. It is more than what you say that counts—IT'S THE WAY YOU SAY IT. Possibly from your very own experience you can recall listening to someone whose VOICE fascinated you—*and for this reason alone you remember that incident,* even though you now forget what was said.

Your own voice can be like that of a well modulated radio, or it can be flat, colorless and uninteresting. Your listeners will react accordingly.

The sad part of it is that *very few of us realize how our voice sounds.* We have heard it so many times that we become accustomed to it. We fail to realize that we may have speaking faults—ALTHOUGH OTHERS RECOGNIZE THEM IMMEDIATELY.

NOW YOU CAN PRACTICE THE SECRETS OF VOICE CONTROL RIGHT IN THE COMFORT AND CONVENIENCE OF YOUR OWN HOME!

No longer must you leave your home or office to attend expensive and time-consuming voice classes. Now, for the first time, I offer you an opportunity to cultivate, right at home in your spare time, *a vivid and compelling voice that will attract and hold the attention of your listeners.* Only 10 to 15 minutes a day is all you need with the famous FREEMANTLE SYSTEM OF VOICE CONTROL.

It's easy! It's fun! My unique system of Voice Control consists of a complete series of 10 lessons in permanently bound book form, plus 6 twelve-inch, R.C.A. Victor records, double-faced, unbreakable.

First you study each lesson at your convenience, then you play the records and listen while I demonstrate the points brought out in each lesson.

It's just like receiving my personal, private instruction right at the Institute itself, *but at a fraction of the cost!*

After you have learned to apply the principles given you in the lessons, you will discover a richness and resonance in your voice that you never before thought possible. *Best of all, you will notice a greater willingness on the part of others to listen to what you have to say.*

TALK YOUR WAY TO SUCCESS! What I offer you today is the opportunity to LEARN HOW TO USE YOUR VOICE so that you'll get more out of life. This tested and proved system is completely different from anything else available. *It is a training program based on sound physical and psychological principles.*

Think back to recent motion pictures or plays you have seen. Remember the voices of those who played the more refined or cultured parts? Their voices had the richer, the lower, the more vibrant tones. YOUR VOICE CAN HAVE THESE SAME FINE QUALITIES.

Decide today that you want to improve your speaking voice. Open the way to bigger, better things in life. Turn now to the enclosed folder and see for yourself the many personal and monetary advantages possible if you are honestly determined to correct your speaking faults.

MAIL THE ENCLOSED ENROLLMENT BLANK TODAY. You need send only $7.50 now, then only $5 a month for six months. That's all you pay for the complete set of instructions, including my book and the six records. If you prefer, you may send $32.50 now in full payment, thus saving $5. In either case, you must be entirely satisfied, or you may return both book and records within 7 days for full refund of every dollar you paid.

But don't wait another minute to take this important step. Fill in and mail the enrollment blank TODAY.

Cordially,

Letters to Salesmen

There are a good many different kinds of salesmen and different occasions for writing them. All we can do here is to make a few general observations. Some of them will apply in your case, and some will not apply at all. Here they are anyway.

In writing letters from the "house" to salesmen in the field, don't make the mistake of turning on too much pep. Salesmen can get fed up with pep talks very quickly, and you soon defeat your purpose.

Be helpful and interested and sympathetic. Be friendly and natural and human. Treat them as equals, as men you respect and like. Don't preach, don't be "high hat," and don't write just for the sake of "getting a letter off to the salesmen." Give them some worth-while information of some kind, and give it as one man to another, not as sales manager to the hired help on the road. (Go ahead and laugh, but a lot of letters read just that way.) Don't write too often unless you do have something important to say.

Give credit where credit is due—and do it wholeheartedly. If you have to scold a salesman, make him "take it and *like* it."

* * *

There's another type of letter to salesmen that deserves some comment. I mean the letter from a manufacturer to the salesmen of his dealers or jobbers. These fellows are not on the manufacturer's payroll and can't be treated as if they were.

They have not only that company's goods to sell, but the products of many other manufacturers as well. Their time and effort are necessarily divided among these various products. Some get a lot, some just a little, some none at all.

Manufacturers whose sales are dependent upon middlemen have a real educational job to do. Frequently a letter isn't the proper thing to use, a printed house organ in some form or other being a better solution to the problem.

Where letters are indicated, it's well to keep them comparatively short, make them helpful if possible, and write them from the salesman's viewpoint whenever this is practicable. The task of writing will be more difficult, but far more productive, if you'll put yourself in the salesman's place before beginning your letter and say, "In his place, how would I react to a letter of this kind?" The reason I said the job would be more difficult is that you may have to tear up three or four letters before you get one that stands up under the test.

Here's a letter to dealers' salesmen that should have interested them (and did) because it pointed the way to more sales:

"The next selection by the sextet will be—NUFORM INTERCHANGEABLE FACINGS"; the title of the enclosed folder, is not just an idle headline.

The next selection by every dentist you call on, WILL be Nuform Interchangeable Facings if you point out the many advantages in using them. Here are teeth whose superiority is not even debatable, and any professional man or laboratory technician can easily prove that to his own satisfaction by comparison and test.

Your sales job is therefore greatly simplified. It isn't necessary to sell the Facings—just sell the idea of comparing Nuform Interchangeable Facings with ANY others on the market, point for point. *The facings will then sell themselves!* This new broadside is going out now to our entire selected list of dentists and should be followed up by a personal call as promptly as possible.

Letters to Farmers

The analysis of your prospect or customer list, recommended in Chapter One, will help you to break down the word "farmer" so that you know pretty definitely just what kind of chap you're writing to. The word obviously takes in a lot of territory. There are the large operators and the small near-city truck farmers. There are hog raisers and corn growers, poultrymen, cotton growers, fruit farmers, gentlemen-farmers, and just farmers. Each represents a different type with different ideas, different background, different ambitions, and different problems.

For the most part, however, the following observations will prove helpful: The farmer is a careful buyer, not at all anxious to part with his money. He doesn't react favorably to "fine language" but prefers and responds more quickly to plain, open, man-to-man talk. The *personal* note, if sincere, is effective in writing to him. He is very apt to shy away from high-pressure selling (as indeed most people are today); he wants to think the proposition over and decide in his own time. It isn't enough to say "mail back the inquiry card to-day"—you must give a logical reason why it would be to his advantage to do so.

He is impressed more by the experience of real farmers, particularly those somewhat near him, than by statistics compiled by state or Federal governments. He wants and must have full information about the product or service you expect him to buy. He'll read any reasonable amount of details you give him if interestingly presented.

Finally, and this is true no matter what kind of prospect you have but particularly true of the farmer, he will respond more readily if your argument is couched in terms of benefit to him rather than if it features your product, factory, or methods.

Notice how this letter to farmers talks the farmers' language—

Having a dairy herd, stock, or poultry, you convert mill feeds, local hay, grain, and grass into the concentrated market products—milk, meat, and eggs. The price you get for these products is controlled by forces beyond your command. The amount of profit depends entirely upon your cost of production.

No one factor in your production costs is more vital than that of feed. You can assure yourself of an animal's ability to produce, through breeding records. You can give it proper housing and care. You can adopt modern methods of sanitation. Then—you can sacrifice all these advantages and greatly reduce the profits you *should* make, by not using the right feed.

Here is where the Eshelman Organization and the Eshelman line of guaranteed feeds can be of real value to you. For 89 years—four generations—Eshelman have been developing and improving and testing farm feeds; working with the interest and background of practical farmers, to bring to you and other feeders a balanced ration that will make feeding more profitable for dairy, livestock and poultry.

There are two ways to prove the economy and value of a feed. No. 1: Test it on a selected stock at a so-called "testing farm."

No. 2: Make that feed prove its worth on the average farm, with average flocks and herds, under average conditions. Eshelman has always believed in practical proof. Feeders have told us that Eshelman Feed produces more profitable results at lower cost, even when compared with other feeds tested on prize stock.

On the next two pages you will find some of these results described. You can be sure that whatever your feeding requirements, there is an Eshelman Guaranteed Feed scientifically and uniformly prepared to bring profitable results. Go to your Eshelman dealer and get a few bags. Try this good feed on your stock. We feel sure you will do as other feeders have done for many years—come back for more Eshelman Feed because it makes more money for you.

Letters to Inactive Customers

This is about the business graveyard—that desolated land of lost customers where the dead may be made to rise again *if* you push the right button.

Before we get into that, let's discuss the question of what made these accounts die out and become inactive. What did you do to them to "kill" them so far as business for you is concerned?

Just as every company receives a certain amount of business without any apparent effort, so it likewise loses a certain amount the same way. Business drifts in and drifts out, and for these changes in the sales volume no credit or blame can be attached to you.

In both cases, however, that applies to the smallest part of the total volume. You get the major portion of your business because you've earned it, and you lose the major portion of your *inactive* customers because you deserve to.

If you could make a study of all your correspondence during the past few years, you'd probably find that some letters were tactless, some were antagonistic and curt, some were critical and superior, and some, perhaps, were downright nasty. Notice I say *some*. How many that represents varies with every business, but the chances are that the size of your "graveyard" will be in direct proportion to the number of these letters in your files.

It is so easy to drive away business through everyday correspondence that you just don't realize you're doing it.

Take an opening paragraph like this, for instance:

Dear Mr. Brown:

We have written you three times during the past months and for some reason you haven't seen fit to reply.

Accusing a man of discourtesy will not bring the two of you any closer together, will it? Here's how it might have been written:

Dear Mr. Brown:

I wonder if you'll be good enough to do me a favor? I must have "fallen down" completely in my attempt to tell you our proposition or I would certainly have heard from you by now.

* * *

Here's another type that gets a fellow's back up:

Dear Mr. Brown:

In looking over our files, I find that we haven't received any orders from you for sixteen months. Why is this, Mr. Brown?

The writer sounds grieved and antagonistic, which tends only to make the inactive customer glad he is inactive. Here's another way of saying the same thing.

Dear Mr. Brown:

Have you, in your business, ever had a good customer suddenly stop buying, without any apparent reason? Well, that's the predicament I'm in now.

* * *

Then there's the letter that starts off in a critical or superior sort of manner:

Dear Mr. Brown:

That old-fashioned filing system of yours is losing money for you every day in the week. Did you realize that?

"Trying to tell me how to run my business, eh? Well, you can tell those folks, etc., etc." Here's one way to express the same thought with finesse:

Dear Mr. Brown:

You've heard of the H. A. Snowden Company? Well, they told me just last Thursday that the eliminating of their old filing system meant a decrease in overhead of 20 per cent the first year.

These are only examples, of course. They illustrate but a very few of many different ways in which the letter writer can lose business. One way, therefore, to curtail the size of your company's "graveyard" is carefully to search each letter, before you sign it, for anything and everything that might *rub the wrong way*.

How about going down to the "graveyard" of inactive customers to see if we can't bring some of them back to life?

First, why are they "dead"? For either of two reasons—because of something you did or something someone else did. Either a member of your organization rubbed them the wrong way—by letter, wire, telephone or in person—or a competitor told them an attractive story about price, quality, service, or whatnot that made your proposition seem like the second best. Therefore, let's divide the inactive file into different groups and treat them accordingly.

You will probably find that there are some cases where you can pretty well lay your finger on the trouble. You *know* that those in this group have drifted to another firm because of price or service or for some other reason touching on price, quality, or service that you feel was beyond your control.

You will find others that can definitely be traced through your file of complaints. There are cases where the customer is inactive because of some real or imaginary grievance.

Group 1 consists of lost customers who are inactive because they have been sold on the idea of buying elsewhere.

Group 2 are the lost customers who have been antagonized by some unintended display of tactlessness, discourtesy, anger, or indifference.

Group 3 are the lost customers about whom you know

nothing, except that for some unknown reason they stopped buying.

Thus we have them classified, and are ready to work on them. A series of three letters to each group would be one effective method of planning the campaign.

In a general way, Group 1 should be handled with a formidable array of sales arguments to convince the ex-customer that he is missing something—in price, quality, or service—by not buying from you.

Group 2 should be approached with the one idea of straightening out the complaint. In some cases you will decide that an apology or explanation is necessary before the customer would think of buying from you again. In other cases you will decide that opening up the wound would do more harm than good. (In making that decision, however, bear in mind the fact that little wrinkles frequently stay wrinkles until they are ironed out and that many times a reconciliation is impossible until the grievance is satisfactorily eliminated.)

Group 3 should receive *sounding-out* letters, written with only one thought in mind—to find out, in a nice way, just why the customer has stopped buying.

The following letter is an example of one appeal that could be used on this group:

Do you feel the same way I do about these so-called "inactive" accounts?

If you do—you don't like them—at least until you know the reason why they are inactive.

The gadgets which you have bought from us in the past were, to the best of my knowledge, the finest possible to make. They were priced right, I know, for our margin is exceedingly small. And we certainly tried to give you A-1 service.

What I'd like to know—and what you would want to know in my place—is why aren't we serving you now?

In short, we have what I believe you want and need—at the right price. Won't you please indicate your requirements on the enclosed card and let us quote you? I'm anxious to place your name where it rightfully belongs—on our *active* customer list—and I think you'll appreciate having it there.

Whatever letters you write, write them from the other fellow's standpoint. Don't let even the slightest feeling of antagonism creep in. Be friendly, courteous, and interested in *his* problems as well as your own. In a nutshell, look at it from *his* side of the fence and make him look at it from yours.

CHAPTER NINE

Pointers on Specific Types of Letters

Letters Written to Get Inquiries

An inquiry is what makes the difference between a "suspect" and a "prospect." It is the first step in the selling of many different products and services. An inquiry is really just a nibble, a tug at the line, a dip of the bob—in other words, an expression of curiosity. Good inquiries in the business world are worth their weight in gold, for they constitute "live leads" and the percentage of them that can be turned into orders is frequently quite high. Notice that I said *"good inquiries."*

Therefore the problem of how to secure them, or how to secure more of them, is an important one. Broadly speaking, there are two ways to solicit inquiries by letter—a direct way and a roundabout way.

The Direct Way. The direct way attempts to arouse interest in the product or proposition so that the prospect will be impelled to send back a return card asking for further details. There are two serious mistakes that are frequently made in connection with this type of letter. One is to give too much information, so much that the recipient has no incentive to write back. He *thinks* he knows all about the product and will decide (most of the time unfavorably for you) on the

strength of that information. The second mistake is not making any provision for return of the inquiry.

Here is a letter that was unsuccessful because it committed
both crimes.

Did you know that you can purchase lining plates for
your ball and tube mills for just half the price which you
have been paying; which would last three times as long,
give greater production, cut down your expenses by not
having to close the plant as often for repairs? Wouldn't
you consider giving such lining plates some consideration
if they have all these essential qualifications?

We do manufacture such grinding plates and our
foundry will be glad to convince you by offering you an
eight months' extension to pay the last half of your in-
voice. Unless we really did manufacture liners of such
merit, we could not begin to grant such terms.

Our foundry fully realizes that output depends upon
the employed metal, the harder the surface, the better it
will grind; the longer it will keep its shape; the less it
will wear away; and that the lesser the friction the purer
and greater will be the ground material. The lining
plates manufactured by our works meet in every respect
these essential conditions and are cast out of our NEO
metal, a secret formula, with special extra-hard chilled
working surfaces, Brinell hardness in the chilled parts
450 to 475.

All we ask is a sketch showing the weight, size, thick-
ness, number of pieces, and our lining plates can be delivered to your mill one month from receipt of your
order. We quote $5\frac{3}{4}\cent$ a pound of 2000 pounds to the ton
f.o.b. American docks, rail freight your account.

We are assuming all the risk for our liners and if they
do not meet in every respect our foundry's guarantee,

relative to the above-mentioned conditions, you may send them back at our expense.

Why not take advantage of our unusual offer now and equip your plant with our liners? Trusting that you will give us the courtesy of a reply, we remain

Here is a letter that attempts to do nothing more than arouse interest, bring out a need for the product, and supply the prospect with an incentive or motive for looking further:

It will be to your interest to test every table in your dining room for wobble and unsteadiness.

The old-fashioned makeshift method of steadying a table with a folded piece of paper or sliver of wood is not in keeping with the up-to-dateness of your club or with the trend of the times.

The new and *better* way is with "Adjusta" casters or glides. Put them in and say good-bye forever to all embarrassment, disorder and inconvenience that result so frequently from a wobbly table.

You may not have noticed it, but you probably have lost the good-will of some of your members—every club restaurant has—through the spilling of coffee, soup, gravy, etc.—accidents that are not your fault at all, but that of an unsteady table.

The investment required to equip your tables with "Adjustas" is small—the dividends, in more enjoyment and less annoyance for your members, will wipe out the cost in a very short time.

Use the card, please, to request prices and complete information.

The direct way of getting an inquiry is recommended where the inquiry can be followed by a personal call or where the sales argument is a comparatively simple one.

The Roundabout Way. This method is effective when the best approach is an appeal to curiosity alone or where the sales presentation is so involved as to require the help of a booklet or other literature to "put the story across."

The so-called "teaser" letter uses the roundabout way of getting an inquiry. The letter might not even mention the product or service being sold. For instance:

> How would you like to cut your office overhead 40% without in any way sacrificing production?
>
> We have developed a plan that I can guarantee will do just that.
>
> If you will tell me a convenient time on the enclosed card, I shall be very glad to explain how—without obligating you in the least bit.

Wouldn't *you* send back the return card, if the letter seemed to come from a reliable company?

In writing this kind of letter, appealing to curiosity alone, be sure that you include a *motive* for replying; be sure you make your letter sound sincere and be sure you can properly satisfy the prospect's curiosity after you have aroused it.

The roundabout way is also used where the sales story is long and complicated, where graphs, charts, illustrations, testimonials, etc., are called for—in other words, where a booklet must be depended upon to do a large part of the selling.

The object of the letter in this case is not to sell the prospect on the product but *on the idea of writing for the booklet.* In preparing the booklet, it is wise to put into it information valuable to the prospect, so that it can be effectively merchandised.

The following letter (one of a series of follow-ups) aims at getting the prospect to write for the booklet, in the hope that the booklet story, in pictures and words, will be impressive and convincing enough to do a selling job.

Just two fast questions and you can get on with your busy day—

1. Do you use outdoor signs?
2. Would you like to reduce your sign costs? I don't mean with cheaper signs. I mean with signs that sell *longer*.

If your answer to those questions is yes, you should be interested in a 20-page brochure that not only tells you how to get greater sign mileage—it PROVES it!

It tells you why du Pont, Champion, Goodrich, Coca-Cola, Shell Oil, Cadillac and many other discriminating companies use Allen-Morrison signs . . . and the specific reasons why they find them an outstanding investment.

It tells you what to look for when you buy signs, how to get the maximum mileage from whatever signs you use.

May we send you a copy, with our compliments? No charge—no obligation—mail the request card today.

Whether the direct way or the roundabout way of soliciting inquiries is adopted—and which you use will depend, of course, upon the job to be done—it is usually advisable to follow up those who don't respond.

That means planning a definite campaign of letters, and I mean *really planning*. First set down, in the order of their importance, all the appeals that you can honestly say apply to the proposition. With them written down, you will be reasonably sure of not overlooking any. Plan your follow-up letters now so that you use *all* your ammunition, highlighting all the various features and benefits to be derived from the use of the product or service.

The interval between mailings can be anywhere from a few days to a week or ten days in the beginning of the campaign, to possibly a month or longer between mailings later on.

As to the number of follow-ups to include in your campaign, send as many letters as you feel from past experience can be sent *profitably*. The selling price and the margin of profit will, of course, be important factors in setting up your plan. Generally speaking, the higher the price of the product or service, the greater can be the interval between mailings and the more mailings sent. Keep in mind when writing follow-up letters that the reason for the follow-up lies in the failure of the first letter to bring an inquiry. If you remember that, you will send out better and more effective follow-up letters, because you will realize that, if the argument used in the first letter didn't produce the desired action, then certainly the same argument won't click in the second. Incidentally, in most cases, it is neither necessary nor advisable to make reference in your follow-up to those letters which have gone before.

Letters Written to Answer Inquiries

You have the inquiry now. The question is how to answer it—how to turn it into a sale. There are a few fundamental rules that it will pay you to follow.

Make sure that the inquirer's name and address are spelled correctly in your answering letter. There is nothing I know of that can so effectively start a well-written letter on its way to the wastebasket as garbling the salutation. Make the letter as personal looking as possible. If you are answering inquiries on such a large scale that individual typing is impractical, use electrically typewritten letters or good filled-in multigraphed letters. A sloppy-looking circular letter will dampen the prospect's interest.

Start your letter by thanking the prospect for his inquiry or in some way showing your appreciation for his request. This isn't essential, but it does get your story off to a good start.

Tie in with the appeal you used in the original letter, which was successful in arousing his interest in the first place. You hit a vulnerable spot then—*hit it again*.

Be *complete* in your answer. Knock down all the objections that might arise in his mind. Anticipate all the doubts and satisfy them before they have a chance to cause trouble. Assume you know nothing about the product, and supply all the information that you yourself would want in order to make *you* buy.

Send the catalog, booklet, or other printed literature along with your letter, *not under separate cover*. There are numerous duplex envelopes that will carry your letter first class and the other material third class, but all together.

If possible, size up the needs of your prospect, and in your letter adapt your product or service to those needs. The same letter to every inquiry will not generally produce maximum returns.

Get your answering letter off the same day the inquiry is received. It doesn't pay to let a live lead cool off. Strike while the iron is hot. Here is an answer to an inquiry that did—and was successful.

THANK YOU FOR YOUR REQUEST

We are very glad indeed to send you the enclosed sample card.

Since hand weaving is an art and the finished piece a prized possession, we know you'll be interested in the quality of Ederlin—and why it will make your work even more beautiful.

Ederlin is made to meet the requirements of hand

weavers like yourself. And it is made only of *long line fibres*.

If you've ever seen flax spun into yarn, you'll know what that means. The flax goes thru a series of combings, each one finer than the last. By the time it is combed for the last time, all the tow or short fibre is removed. Only the long, glossy fibres remain, fibres that look rich as silk. It is from these long fibres that Ederlin is made. The resulting yarn is lustrous and strong. It is the *quality linen yarn from which heirlooms are made.*

As you can see, there are many beautiful shades of Ederlin besides the natural, bleached and grey line. Ederlin is dyed right here in our own mill so we can assure you that only the best fast colors are used.

You'll probably be anxious to get started on your next piece of weaving as soon as possible. So if you'll fill out the order form and mail it today, we'll see that your Ederlin is shipped promptly.

Here's another good answer to inquiries—

Here is the information on SILVERFILE you inquired about, also information on related products such as SILVERSAFE, SILVERGUARD and SHINEMASTER.

For a limited time, we are offering some very attractive sales-builders that should, if used, boost your volume.

Here they are:

    1—A SILVERFILE counter display rack, as illustrated, *FREE* WITH THE INITIAL PURCHASE of 6 assorted SILVERFILES-SILVERSAFES.

    2—Sturdy self-service SILVERGUARD display, holds 72 SILVERGUARDS, *FREE* WITH INITIAL PURCHASE OF 1 SILVERGUARD unit assortment.

    3—100 SHINEMASTER samples with folder, as enclosed, FREE WITH EACH CASE OF 8 Display Units. Also EXTRA 10% ALLOWED on purchase of 1 case or more.

4—500 SILVERFILE Folders, as enclosed, FREE WITH EACH PURCHASE of 18 units of SILVERFILES and SILVERSAFES. (Charge for imprinting $5.00 per M.)

5—Newspaper ad mat FREE (ad reprint enclosed).

These products are being advertised to over fifty million readers this year. Inquiries are coming in by the hundreds and these are immediately directed to our dealers.

Here's a line that is packaged and styled to stimulate impulse buying at point of sale.

We can ship at once. May we fill your order?

Letters to Follow Up Inquiries

How many to send? As many as you can mail and still make it pay. That might call for one or a dozen—or even more. Making follow-up letters pay depends primarily on two things, consistency and conviction.

Follow-up letters should be mailed at regular intervals, ranging from a day or two to a month or longer, depending on the product or proposition. The higher the price of the product, by and large, the more follow-ups you can send, but the interval between them should be greater. That statement may require an explanation. In selling a piano, for instance, the margin of profit is large enough to permit of, say, twelve or more follow-up letters, the first three a week apart and the rest at intervals of a month.

In selling a low-priced specialty, on the other hand, the profit may be such that the use of more than two or three follow-ups would be questionable—and certainly the spark of

interest originally aroused wouldn't survive an interval between mailings of more than a few days.

In writing this type of letter, keep these things in mind:

1. Remember, he didn't respond for some reason or other,
as the result of your first letter and the information you sent
him. So the chances are it won't do you much good to bawl
him out for not replying—however gently—or just to remind
him that you sent the information and are wondering whether
or not he is ready to take action.

No, you almost have to start over, creating interest, whet-
ting the appetite, building up the benefits and advantages.
You have a *sales* job to do.

2. He probably *won't want to read* this follow-up letter
you're writing. If he has received and read the original letter
and the descriptive literature which no doubt accompanied it,
he *thinks* he knows all about your product or service now.
That's why your opening sentence is so important. It must
almost force the reader into the body of the letter. Here are
some opening paragraphs that *do*—

> There is one point in my recent letter that I partic-
> ularly want to emphasize, because it is important to *you*.

> Did you notice in the material I sent you last week in
> answer to your request, the GUARANTEE on page 4 of the
> folder?

> Here is another phase of our service that I believe you
> would find helpful.

Whatever your personal opinion of testimonials, bear in
mind that, properly used, they have always been effective.
My prediction is that they always will be. What experience
someone else has had with your product is of the utmost importance to a prospective buyer. Notice how effectively testimonials are used in this letter:

NEW . . . DIFFERENT . . . *NOT* A REDUCING COMPOUND
—DOES NOT HURT GLOSS . . . INCREASES SCRATCH
RESISTANCE

Anti-Offset Compound #WC-50
really STOPS offset in printing
—stops sticking in the piles!

TRY THIS NEW ANTI-OFFSET COMPOUND WITHOUT
FINANCIAL RISK!

Read what important paper box manufacturers say about the new Glenn-Killian Anti-Offset Compound #WC-50:

From Chicago, Illinois

"We tried the sample of your Compound #WC-50 on a press run. Please RUSH us a 30 lb. order!"

From Los Angeles, Calif.

"When we received your TRIAL ORDER of Anti-Offset Compound #WC-50, we sent it to our own laboratory for testing. They reported that it 'looked good' to them. We then tried it on a regular press run. It was not only *good*, it is by far the best thing we've ever used to prevent offset and sticking in the piles. Please send us a 30 gallon drum immediately."

From Baltimore, Md.

"Just tried your sample of Anti-Offset Compound #WC-50. Are holding up a big order until we get more. Please send 50 lbs. by *special delivery*."

And there are many, many more! In every paper box plant where Anti-Offset Compound #WC-50 has been tried, it has been enthusiastically accepted!

NOW YOU CAN TRY IT YOURSELF ON THIS
SPECIAL NO-RISK TRIAL OFFER:

Here's all you do: First, use the enclosed post-paid card to order a 5 lb. Trial Can of Anti-Offset Compound #WC-50. We will ship your order immediately. Then, try the compound *in your regular ink on a regular press run.*

Anti-Offset Compound #WC-50 is a thin wax paste. You just mix it into your ink—either by hand or by machine—in the commercial proportions of 1–1½ *ounces* of compound to one *pound* of ink. Then use the ink as you always do.

When we send you your trial order of compound, we will also bill you at the regular price of $6.25 for 5 lbs. BUT . . . if you are not *completely* satisfied that Anti-Offset Compound #WC-50 does everything we say it will —*stops* offsetting of ink—*stops* sticking in the piles— if you are not satisfied that it does these things, then send back the bill with a note to that effect. In other words, *if you don't like it, you don't have to pay for it!*

Of course, we think you will like Compound #WC-50. We're so certain of it, that when we bill you for the 5 lb. Trial Can, we will also send you an order form with our discount prices for quantity orders. That way, when you pay the bill, you can also order an additional quantity for immediate shipment.

So don't delay in finding out about this amazing new Anti-Offset Compound—*the first Anti-Offset Compound that really works.* Fill out the enclosed card and get it in the mail right now—no postage is needed.

When sending descriptive literature with your follow-ups, it is good practice to use the letter to create interest in the booklet or folder and let the printed piece, with its color, illustration, headlines, and text matter, do the actual selling.

Don't feel that it is necessary in follow-up letters to make reference to those which have preceded it, and don't under any circumstances allow even the slightest hint of reproach to creep into your copy. I have seen letters start out this way:

WE DO NOT UNDERSTAND, GENTLEMEN . . .

Thus began a bad follow-up to an inquiry. It was in the form of a headline leading into the following first paragraph—

why, after you inquired regarding our products—and we wrote you fully sending you prices, etc.—we have not had the pleasure of receiving and filling an order for you.

It *shouldn't* be hard to understand why the inquirer hasn't sent in an order. *He wasn't sold.* Or he just hasn't gotten around to it yet. Or he had no intention of ordering in the first place. Was just curious.

In any event, he won't be moved to action by a follow-up like this one. Look on *your* follow-up letters as *continuations* of the selling process. Apparently what was said in the first answer to the inquiry wasn't appealing enough to this particular prospect to make him want to buy. Okay, you can't sell *everybody* on the first call. Trot out some more potent sales arguments. Keep on selling in your second, third and all subsequent tries. Remember, each follow-up should be *stronger*, not weaker, because it has an increasingly difficult job to do.

Here's another example of how *not* to start a follow-up letter—

Gentlemen:

We have written to you from time to time regarding our National radio program designed to reach the Negro market covering especially the states of Texas, Louisiana,

Florida, Mississippi, Missouri, North Carolina, South
Carolina, Alabama, Georgia, Tennessee, Arkansas, Okla-
homa, Kansas, Illinois, Indiana, Ohio, Virginia, Ken-
tucky, West Virginia and New Mexico. This program is
on the air every Wednesday night over the powerful
Station XEG, Monterrey, Mexico.

You'll agree this first paragraph is too long, is made uninteresting by the long list of states, says *nothing* that would
make the recipient *want* to read further.

When you have received all that you can from your list of
inquiries, before you throw it into the discard, try one more
letter, a *good* letter, offering some special inducement to buy.
This last squeeze might surprise you.

Letters to Present Customers

I don't care how old and threadbare the saying is, I must
use it here: It costs less to *keep* a customer than to get a new
one. Another favorite, and just as true: *Your* customer is the
other fellow's prospect. Depend on it that there isn't a customer on your books who isn't being peppered all the time
with advertising missiles from one or more of your competitors.

Admit then that an important part of your selling should
be directed toward cementing relations with customers.

What kind of letter should go to them? This is hard to tell
without knowing what kind of business is concerned, but
these points hold true in any event:

1. Letters should be fairly personal. Certainly you can
afford to be personal with someone who buys from you.

2. They should go out at regular intervals, and they should
keep going out indefinitely. You can't ever stop working on
customers to *keep them customers.*

3. They should do a selling job, strengthening the confidence the customer has in you and in your product or service.

4. They should be informative, educational, or helpful, if possible, in order to justify reading.

5. They might (not necessarily *should*) ask the customer for names of friends or relatives who could also enjoy the advantages of the product.

Letters to Bring Back Old Customers

If you are in business, undoubtedly you have some inactive customers on your books. Do you know why they are inactive? Do you know why they stopped buying? I'll tell you.

Some have *passed away* to another world. Some have *moved away,* out of your field of operation. Some have been *wooed away* by a competitor. Some have been *scared away* by the discourteous treatment of one of your employees or by a tactless statement of one of your correspondents. Some have been *forced away,* by circumstances that make it economically necessary for them to buy on a cheaper basis than you sell.

The questions are, do you know *which* of these reasons applies to which customers and do you know which reason predominates? The more you know about this phase of your business, the fewer inactive customers you'll have.

Pointers on how to write to them? Again, it's hard to be very specific without knowing the business, but these thoughts might help:

1. Try to find out in which of the above classifications the customer belongs. If necessary, come right out and ask him.

2. Admit the possibility of grounds for complaint, and offer to adjust it.

3. Do a reselling job on your product, service, or proposition.

4. Offer some inducement, if necessary, for coming back into the fold.

5. Be as personal as you can and still keep your letter sincere.

More on the subject of regaining lost customers will be found on page 113.

Letters to Pave the Way for Salesmen's Call

The object of a letter of this kind is to make the work of the salesman easier. Any man calling on "cold turkey" exclusively has a tough job. In nearly every case, the biggest percentage of people he calls on will not be interested and will tell him so in no uncertain terms. It's discouraging work.

In order to cut down the percentage of those not interested, many companies precede the calls of their men with one or more letters, so that the prospect will be at least partially sold when the salesman arrives.

In writing such letters, keep in mind that your letter doesn't have to stand entirely on its own feet. It is now part of a "doubles team" where teamwork is the order of the day.

A letter trying to do too much of the selling job can do more harm than good. Don't take away all the salesman's ammunition. Leave him enough at least to use in closing the sale.

Therein lies the secret to writing letters that pave the way for a salesman's call. Make them really pave the way; make them really tie in with his call; make them a *help* rather than a *hindrance*.

The one big object of this type of letter is to put the prospect in a frame of mind in which he will (1) be willing or curious to see the salesman and hear what he has to say, (2) be glad to see the salesman or (3) be so doggone anxious to see him that he can't wait. The degree to which you attain these results is the yardstick for measuring the success of your efforts.

Letters to Follow Up Salesmen's Calls

The salesman, in this instance, has made the call. He didn't come away with an order, nor did he get a flat turndown. What can be done to sustain and increase the interest aroused by the salesman? Letters can do the job for you very nicely if you use the right kind.

Talk with your salesmen, and find out the main points of resistance that they run into. If there is just one—price, for instance—write your follow-up letters around that angle, proving to the prospect that your product or service is the least expensive by reason of its finer performance, better quality, etc. If there are several points of resistance, you might deliberately plan your series of follow-up letters around them.

Use "reason-why" copy if possible. Bring in all the *proof* you can lay your hands on to back up the claims made by your representative. Testimonials in this kind of letter are very often effective if they are authentic and believable.

Remember, if the salesman with all the advantages of personal selling couldn't win over the customer, it's a cinch you can't do it with wishy-washy letters. You *can* do it in many cases, however, with interesting, convincing letters that wear away resistance like drops of water on a stone.

Letters to Sell in between the Calls of Salesmen

This is frequently done over the salesman's signature. It is an excellent means of keeping in touch with customers and prospects who aren't important enough to justify continual personal contact at short intervals.

In some businesses, the best customers must be called on

once a week. Certainly they require no letter writing in between. The potential or actual business of another group justifies personal calls perhaps once a month, but much good can be done with the right kind of letter sent at the halfway mark.

Such letters can be order-seeking or of the keep-in-touch variety, depending on circumstances. In either case, they should keep the efforts of the salesman in mind and tie in with them, not compete with them.

If the letter seeks an order, be sure you give sufficient reason why the order should be forthcoming. And if the purpose is simply to keep in touch with the prospect or customer until the salesman gets around again, be sure you don't waste the man's time, or the salesman, when he turns up, may get a cool reception.

Don't just "get out a letter." If you can't make your message actually helpful, make it informative; if you can't do that but still have to write a letter, at least make it interesting. This type of letter, speaking generally, should be on the short side.

Letters to Get Testimonials

Surprising to say, many companies have no file marked "Testimonial Letters." They've never thought about it, never got around to it, or just didn't realize what a golden opportunity they were missing.

Right here, let me quote from a well-known authority, who in discussing testimonials wrote:

> He is not a good letter writer who tries to tell the story himself when he could induce satisfied customers to help him tell it.

Testimonials are extremely valuable if only as a source of supply for sales ammunition. The way to get them, if an insufficient number of them come unsolicited, is to write for them.

Don't write a long letter—it isn't necessary—and don't fail to enclose a self-addressed, stamped envelope if you want the maximum number of returns. Here's the type:

> I wonder if you'll be good enough to do me a small favor. It won't take you but a few minutes.
>
> You have been using one of our so-and-sos for about a year now and I have every reason to believe you have been well pleased with it.
>
> If that's true (and if it isn't, I want to know it), I would consider it a real kindness if you'd drop me a note telling just what your experiences have been—what kind of work it has done, how it has stood up, how the men in your plant like it, etc., etc.
>
> Would you do that for me? I'll appreciate it a lot if you will and will surely reciprocate in some way if I can.
>
> A self-addressed, stamped envelope is enclosed, and, if it would be any more convenient, just use the back of this sheet for your letter. Thanks again.

Letters to Apply for a Job

On this subject, we'd better say first that job seekers should possess the necessary qualifications for filling the position for which they are applying. The best letters possible to write won't make up for a lack of training or ability.

Assuming then that you really believe you can handle the job if you get it, here are some things to keep in mind.

1. The purpose of your letter is not to get the position, but simply an interview at which time you will have ample opportunity to *sell yourself*.

2. Your letter will undoubtedly have plenty of competi-

tion. Interviews will be granted on the basis of how the application letters *stack up*. You'll want yours to *stand out from the crowd*.

3. What you are writing is to all intents and purposes a *sales* letter, selling YOU as the product. The more you visualize the prospective employer and the more you tell of your qualifications and experience from the standpoint of *his* problems, the better your chances for an interview.

4. While putting your best foot forward, don't make "unbelievable" claims about your potential ability. Modesty will get you further than conceit.

5. Don't be "fresh," facetious, or too informal. On the other hand, don't be "stuffy" either. Write a friendly, sincere letter.

6. Be sure the appearance of your letter is an asset. Many men half judge a letter before they even read it. Your letter can *look* as if it came from a high-grade, dependable, forward-thinking person. And it *can* create the opposite kind of impression.

7. Show your letter to two or three disinterested people before you mail it. Their reactions will be helpful.

8. A short letter, with a separate résumé of your experiences and background, is better than a long letter that tells the whole story and takes up two or three pages doing it. The short letter, if properly written, will assure reading of the attached résumé, whereas the long letter might never be finished. A two or three "pager" has a tough job getting itself read.

9. Don't base your appeal on sympathy. Don't discuss salary unless it is to stress the fact that it is a purely secondary consideration. Don't talk about dissatisfaction with your present job; avoid discussing any personal grievances. Don't venture too many opinions, particularly about yourself. Don't waste

the reader's time by telling him a lot of things he already knows.

10. A good job is worth at least one follow-up letter, perhaps more.

11. A letter of appreciation for courtesy shown is advisable after the interview. That always makes a good impression.

Here is a poor application letter—because it contains too much "I":

You did not solicit this application, but I feel that I have something to offer you or else I would not waste your time and mine.

For the past twelve years I have wanted to become an advertising copy-writer. When I came out of college, firms were not taking on young men regardless of ambition or intelligence. Therefore, although circumstances compelled me to work at other jobs, I always had the same goal in mind and worked with the idea that eventually I would get into writing advertising copy.

I have clerked in stores, solicited door-to-door, sold products on established routes, built new routes; sold necessities, sold luxuries, and sold intangibles.

I feel that I have a very excellent knowledge of sales psychology, and a knowledge that only an advertising man with considerable experience can duplicate.

To augment this sales knowledge, I have continued my study of Advertising. I first had a course in Advertising at Villanova College where I was taking a Commerce & Finance course. Later I took a correspondence course from the I.C.S. in Scranton. At the present time I am studying Copy and Campaigns at the Charles Morris Price School in Philadelphia.

I am an average American fellow, being thirty years of age, married, and have one child.

I can produce excellent references from school, friends, and former and present employers.

I should certainly appreciate a personal interview at which time we can go into greater detail as to my qualifications, remuneration, and other necessary subjects.

By way of comparison, here is a good application letter:

Would you be willing to give me the benefit of your judgment and experience?

A couple of years ago, I graduated from Rutgers University. (Business Management Course—3 years Varsity football—President of Rutgers Chapter of Kappa Sigma Fraternity.)

With that academic background and the sales and business training I have since received, it seems there should be some real opportunity somewhere.

To find it, of course, is the thing.

What I seek now is some good advice and I feel sure you could give it to me in a very few minutes.

Naturally, if it develops there is an opportunity in your organization, fine. But I'll be grateful for just your advice.

Here's data you might want to have: Age, 23—single—6'2"—178 pounds—excellent health—willing to leave city.

An interview will certainly be appreciated.

A Complaint That Backfired

Cutting loose with a loud and lusty complaint every once in a while is a good thing. Gives you a chance to let off steam. The fact is, you usually feel better after you've blown your top whether the complaint gets results or not. And occasionally you get the desired relief just from *writing* a nasty letter, without mailing it.

Of course, to indulge in the luxury of a red-hot complaint, you should feel honestly justified in making it. Here is a case where the complainant *wasn't,* and tossed all judgment to the four winds. He felt *abused* and wrote the sort of complaint that could do his cause only harm.

He originally sent a form letter of application to a group of advertising agencies. When they failed to reply, he got mad, wrote this at the top of a carbon of his original letter—"Having sent my résumé around May 29, and receiving no acknowledgement at all, I must conclude that you conduct your business about fifteen years behind the times, as set forth in this analysis. I hardly consider it presumptuous of me to criticize, since you introduced the critical element by ignoring my simple, reasonable and everyday request for job consideration."

Could there be a *quicker* way to kill his chances of getting a job?

Letters of Congratulation

Every day in the week there is an opportunity to say that to someone. *Congratulations!* It's a *nice* word. *You* like to hear it. So does everyone else. John Smith has just been made Chairman of the Board, or President of his company. Bill Jones got a hole-in-one yesterday. Sam Brown became the father of twin girls. In your daily newspaper you'll find any number of stories of community service, personal achievement, civic honor, or some other evidence of individual recognition.

Some of the folks referred to are your customers. A lot of the others are your prospects. Almost all of them are persons whose good will is important to your company. *What an opportunity for some good public relations!*

You *know* in advance that a letter saying congratulations from you will be appreciated. Such letters always come as a pleasant surprise. They always make a lasting impression. You know that the person you are congratulating will read every line of your letter with keen interest because your message deals with the subject closest to his heart—*himself.* Just a few pointers about this kind of letter—

Be sure it is *warm and friendly,* personal both in tone and content.

Be sure it looks and reads like an individual message, *not a form letter.*

Write it promptly, when the news is "hot."

Make it comparatively brief, certainly not long-winded.

Be enthusiastic, sincere. Make your letter sound as though you really enjoyed writing it.

Here is a very simple type of congratulatory letter, but effective nevertheless.

Dear ———:

Congratulations on your recent election to Assistant Vice President and best wishes for future success in your new position!

Cordially,

Here is another, to a man upon his retirement.

Dear ———:

Back in December 1945 when I joined the Association staff—just a tyro in the savings bank field—I received one letter, wishing me success in my new position, from a savings bank president. It made a profound impression on me at the time, and I haven't forgotten it since. *That president was you!*

Now that you are retiring from a long and honorable business life, I should like to be among the first to extend personal best wishes and to express sincere admiration for an outstanding job well done by a fine gentleman.

Your 65 years of estimable service with the Green Point Savings Bank will shine like a beacon of inspiration for the younger men in the savings bank business.

May your future years bring nothing but the utmost in happiness and contentment.

Cordially,

And here is an entirely different kind—

Dear Miss——:

Congratulations upon your selection as president of the Juniper Garden Club of Black River!

Gardening, especially the raising of flowers, is a hobby which adds zest to life. Many businessmen follow this worth-while outdoor activity but do not have the opportunity to enjoy this form of recreation to the fullest. Women can meet during the day and view the gardens they have planted and created. Having others view the fruits of your labors gives you additional pleasure and satisfaction.

The thought has come to me that possibly your club would like to use the facilities of our bank lobby and display window for a flower show. If you are interested, I am sure it can be arranged.

We extend to you, Miss ——, and to your fellow officers and members, our best wishes for a happy and successful year under your leadership.

Sincerely,

CHAPTER TEN *Answers to Letter Questions*

How Should a Letter Be Processed?

There are many different ways to reproduce a letter. Based on cost and appearance, they would line up something like this:

1. By typewriter, either hand- or electrically operated. (See Philadelphia Textile Institute Letter.)

2. A personalized letter done with a paper plate on a multi-lith, then filled in with a carbon paper ribbon on an electric typewriter. (See WCAU Letter.)

3. Multigraphing with a filled-in salutation and signature reproduction. (See Jacob Siegel Letter.)

4. Multigraphing with a headline or fake fill-in. (See Roger Bell Letter.)

5. Printing done with typewriter type on a regular printing press. This type of letter cannot be satisfactorily filled in. (See Pennsylvania Institute of Certified Public Accountants Letter.)

6. Reproduction by offset—photographing the letter and signature and printing on an already printed letterhead. (See Elco Letter.)

7. Mimeographing. (See Philadelphia Magazine Letter.)

8. Reproduction of handwriting. This type of letter is usually printed by offset lithography or reproduced through rubber plates on a multigraph, then personalized with a hand salutation. (See Prep Shop Letter.)

Mr. John Doe
000 Main Street
Centerville, Pennsylvania

Dear Mr. Doe:

As an important part of our Alumni Fund we have been seeking contributions of $100 or more from a group which, through these contributions, forms our Philadelphia Textile Institute Alumni Men of the Year. This list has been expanding but needs to become much larger than it ever has been before.

With a goal of $20,000 a year for the Alumni Fund if only 200 Alumni gave $100 we would exceed our goal with the total of all the lesser contributions. There are many more than 200 alumni who could readily contribute one hundred or more dollars.

Philadelphia Textile Institute has advanced phenomenally in the past few years. Only a visit can convince you of this and you are always welcome. If we are to continue to advance we must have more adequate funds. It is as simple and as important as that. If our Alumni Fund expands we can plan and achieve continued progress. If it does not - but I cannot imagine that our Alumni will permit this sad alternative.

Will you give the fund a boost now by joining our Men of the Year with your check for one hundred or more dollars? It is the early contributors that determine the success of the Fund because their interest stimulates the others and assures success.

Please get us off to a fast start with your check today and earn the thanks of everyone at Philadelphia Textile Institute - your college.

Very truly yours,

Bertrand W. Hayward
President

Enclosure

BWH/rr

OUR GOAL $20,000

WCAU
PHILADELPHIA

CHARLES VANDA
VICE PRESIDENT
IN CHARGE OF TELEVISION

Dear Mr. Bridge:

I'm taking a chance that, in your busy day, you have not had time to see the last issue of U. S. NEWS AND WORLD REPORT. Well, I had the time (though I don't know how), and I came across a feature on television.

It's informative, exciting and certainly one of the most engrossing stories of TV I've ever read. And, because I believe that there must always be a free and friendly exchange of information regarding our favorite subject, I thought it might be nice to pass it along to you.

It's also nice to send you something besides a request for new business - though I don't think I'll overdo it!

Anyway, read it at your leisure, and if you like it, pass it on to some other member of your staff.

Cordially,

Enc.

Charles Vanda

Mr. Harry P. Bridge
Harry P. Bridge Company
1201 Chestnut Street
Philadelphia 7, Pa.

JACOB SIEGEL COMPANY

"The Outercoat House"

NEW YORK OFFICE
200 FIFTH AVE

317 NORTH BROAD STREET

CHICAGO OFFICE
LYTTON BLDG

PHILADELPHIA 7

March 24, 1955

Mr. James Davis
Main & Union Sts.,
Memphis, Tenn.

Dear Mr. Davis:

The Jacob Siegel and Windsor outercoat
lines will be ready for presentation next week.
When you have seen what we have assembled, you
will agree with us, we are sure, that unquestionably we have much to offer to increase your outercoat sales for the coming season.

No stone has been left unturned in an
effort to develop many unique fabric and model ideas.
The Velvet Collar coat for one will play a predomin-
ate part in all clothing operations, and our University model is an unusual adaptation of this idea.
In addition to this you will see various other new
models which will, I dare say, excite you.

I would appreciate if you would drop me a
line at your earliest convenience just when you plan
to come to the market as I would like to show you
these lines personally.

Kindest regards.

Sincerely,

Jack Wilson
Jack Wilson

smf

sponsored by **Journal** *independence square philadelphia 5 pa.*

To all HORMEL salesmen...

HORMEL, as you know, has often been featured in The Bellringer, our Roger Bell Markets merchandising and advertising program. And, even though our stores are an imaginary group, The Bellringer has become a real friend and helper to REAL marketeers.

More than 2,000 of the nation's leading operators--who either own or control the merchandising programs for more than 145,000 stores--receive The Bellringer. As you know, whenever HORMEL advertises in the Journal, they are featured in that month's Bellringer. The enclosed page shows the HORMEL feature which we made from your beautiful August advertisement, "Two SPAMwich Favorites."

All of your good retail customers should appreciate the wonderful sales help this tempting advertisement will give them.

We hope the promotion we're using in our Roger Bell Food Markets will give you some helpful suggestions in planning retail tie-ins for your customers.

                              Good Selling

                              Roger Bell

                              Roger Bell

RB:bap

Pennsylvania Institute

of Certified Public Accountants

Office of the President
1518 Walnut Street, Philadelphia 2

To the Successful Candidates
in the 1955 CPA Examination:

I am writing to congratulate you upon successfully concluding your efforts to pass the examination for certified public accountant in Pennsylvania. I hope you will be equally as successful in meeting the remaining requirements for obtaining the certificate.

The public accounting profession is an honorable one in which each member plays an important part. The integrity and prestige of the profession is affected by the actions of each member. The importance of the proper professional attitude is so great that this year the Pennsylvania Institute of Certified Public Accountants is presenting at the dinners held for successful candidates a copy of a book entitled "The CPA and His Profession".

The efforts of the Pennsylvania Institute of Certified Public Accountants are devoted to the public interest and to the protection and advancement of the interests of the certified public accountants of our Commonwealth. You will, no doubt, consider becoming a member of our organization when you receive your certificate and thereby contribute your efforts to the development of the profession. We shall be glad to have you join us in this work.

In the near future you will receive from the Chairman of the Committee on Membership of the Institute's Chapter in your geographical area a brochure describing the work of the Institute and the benefits to be derived from membership. If you have any questions or wish additional information, I shall be glad to have you write to me.

I wish you a long, successful, and pleasant career and look forward to welcoming you as a member of the profession.

Sincerely yours,

Ralph L. Stauffer

Ralph L. Stauffer
President

RLS:des

ELCO CORPORATION

"M" Street Below Erie Avenue, Philadelphia 24, Pa. :: CUmberland 9-5500
America's Quality Line of Sockets, Shields and World-Famous Varicon Connectors

Dear Shareholder:

Elco Corporation is pleased to welcome you to its growing group of shareholders.

The current fiscal year, which ends on June 30th is a significant one for Elco Corporation. During this year the corporation has offered its stock to the public and entered into an automation program to increase its production. New machines, which have been designed to mechanize successive assembly operations are in the process of construction and delivery. As a matter of fact, several of these machines have already been delivered and are now in use.

New products, namely various types of printed circuit connectors, printed circuit sockets and sub-miniature Varicon connectors have received favorable acceptance and are providing increased sales. The engineering department of the corporation is keeping pace with the rapid advances in electronic components and devices.

The cost of the development of the new products and the new machines will result in lower earnings for the current fiscal year. However, the use of the machines and the increased sales of the new products should reflect satisfactory profits during the next fiscal period.

I have just returned from a successful European selling and buying trip. The export business of the company will be expanded.

The annual financial statement and report of operations will be published and mailed to all shareholders within a few months.

Very truly yours,

ELCO CORPORATION

BENJAMIN FOX,
           President

Architects Building, 17th and Sansom Sts., Philadelphia 3, Pa. LO 7-3800

devoted to the progress of Business, Commerce and Industry

greater **Philadelphia** *magazine*

The trend is swinging to color.

Whatever you do, wherever you go, you can be certain that the successful man is the one who changes with the times — and the switch is to harmony, to color.

The Frank Wolf Company wants to be the first to bring this exciting new trend to your attention. We heartily recommend that you add to your idea folder this perfect blending of stylishly modern office furniture and scintillating new colors.

"We like to work when we like where we're working."

You'll enjoy working in an atmosphere of light, of cleanliness, of <u>COLOR</u>.

For further information may we suggest you contact Mr. Lafair direct at LOcust 7-2303.

Yours truly,

MERCHANDISE DEPARTMENT

GREATER PHILADELPHIA MAGAZINE

encl.

Published in cooperation with the Chamber of Commerce of Greater Philadelphia

"FOR MEN SIX TO SIXTEEN"

The Prep Shop. Inc.

DARTMOUTH AVENUE · SWARTHMORE, PA.

*Sweaters
& Swimwear*
  Robert Bruce

•

Shirts
  Bruxton Prep
  Dan River

•

Underwear
  Reis

•

Knitwear
  Kaynee

•

Dungarees
  Lee

•

Socks
  Nuweave

•

Belts
  Pioneer

•

Rainwear
  U.S. Rubber

•

*Suits, Sport Coats
and Slacks*
  Chips & Twigs

May I invite you to visit our new store in Swarthmore? It is completely stocked with all new-branded merchandise, with sizes ranging from age "six to sixteen."

Many mothers have brought their boys in, and we have discussed their needs both as to price range and styles. I think they now feel confident in our ability to guide them in their selections should they care to "Do it yourself."

You busy mothers therefore, will not be obliged, although you are welcome, to visit us each time your boy needs socks, shirts etc. However for major items, such as suits sport coats and the like, we would appreciate your coming along to help advise us.

The Prep Shop carries a complete line of merchandise. However, any suggestions on additional items, please let us know. Incidentally, you will find most of your camp and summer swimming needs here also.

Our prices are in line — so why travel distances when we are in your own back yard!

If you want to call, the telephone number is Kingswood 4-0884.

Sincerely,
Cld. Carney

The question as to which of these ways should be adopted for any particular letter campaign depends on the kind of product, on the size and character of the list, on the nature of the proposition, on how important it is to carry out the illusion of a personal letter.

In some cases, it is highly essential that the prospect be made to think that the letter he is receiving is a strictly personal one. Sometimes the use of a personal letter is a mark of business courtesy that the prospect (the president of a large corporation, for instance) would have a right to expect. In both instances, an individually typewritten or electrically typewritten letter should be used.

There are many other situations where you have no desire to "kid" the prospect into thinking that he is the only one receiving your letter but where your own pride demands that your letter live up to a high standard of appearance. Also, there are many cases where you want a personalized effect but the size of the list or the expense budget will not justify either typewriting or mechanical processing. In both situations, the right answer is a multigraphed letter with carefully filled-in salutation.

Next in the scale is the same letter multigraphed, printed, or lithographed, without the fill-in—left out primarily because the proposition will not stand the cost. Then comes mimeographing at still lower cost.

A fairly safe rule to follow is: The higher the type of list and the more expensive the product or service, the more necessary it is to approach as closely as possible a personally typewritten letter.

Do Filled-in Letters Pay?

They do, providing they produce for you a more profitable percentage of returns than the same letter not filled in. Divide your list into two sections; send filled-in letters to half and unfilled-in letters to the other half. The result will give you the only accurate answer to the question.

A more helpful answer would be to say that, on very large lists, a fill-in isn't usually practical because it slows up production. Few of the so-called volume mailers would use a fill-in even if it did result in a slightly higher return, because for one thing they probably wouldn't be able to get out as many mailings and for another the increased cost might easily offset the increased result, if any. The smaller the list, the greater the need for considering whether or not to use fill-ins. Sometimes it works out to advantage; other times, not.

What Kind of Postage Should Be Used?

In answering, I shall have to call again on my good friend, General Lee Speaking, because nothing but a general answer to the question can be given. Usually, the advantage in first-class mail depends upon the unit of sale. It is recommended for letters to comparatively small lists when the product or service is high-priced. It is *not* recommended as having any advantage in pulling power for letters to very large lists when low-priced products or services are being sold.

Those sending letters about medium-priced products to small and medium-sized lists will have to experiment and find out for themselves which type of postage, first or third, produces the most profitable returns.

You will find all kinds of conflicting opinions on the subject. One man will tell you he never even opens the envelope of a third-class letter. Another will tell you that he opens all envelopes anyway so that the postage couldn't make any difference. A third will give you the result of a test showing that first-class postage outpulled third class by one and a half to one. And a fourth will tell you about a test *he* made in which he got just as many returns with third-class postage as with first, at, of course, a very much lower cost.

Naturally, there is a slight psychological advantage in favor of first-class postage. The question is whether the advantage, as reflected in actual results, is great enough to warrant the extra cost.

The only way to find out is to make a test. Don't, however, make the mistake of dividing the list in half and using first-class postage on one group and third-class on the other. That wouldn't be fair because the cost of mailing in one case is much less than the other. Spend the same amount of money on each side.

Be sure also that everything else is equal. The letter inside the envelope should be the same in every detail. In using third-class postage, it is well to remember that many companies employ mail clerks, who open and distribute all letters regardless of postage. For that reason, since the reader might not know what kind of postage was used, favorable action will often depend on the impression made by the letterhead, the mechanical appearance of the letter, the interest aroused by the first paragraph, the desire created by the following paragraphs, the motive that is employed, and all the other essential requirements. So, regardless of postage used, don't neglect any of them if you want your letter to enjoy maximum returns.

What about Return Postage?

This is a much disputed question and one that must be answered individually for each person. What has been said about testing the use of first- and third-class postage applies also to the various methods that are available for encouraging an inquiry or order.

Whether to enclose a business-reply envelope with a permit, an addressed envelope with a stamp on it, a business-reply card with permit, a government postal card or a private mailing card for the prospect to stamp, or none at all depends entirely on circumstances and can be determined with accuracy only by a test.

I can be definite on one point, at least: *Making it easy and convenient for the prospect to reply is one of the fundamentals of mail selling.* Which method will give you best results is a matter of experiment, but you need no experimenting to know that *one* of those methods is better than none. You are almost certain to get more inquiries or orders back if you provide the means; from my experience anyway, you should receive enough more to make the return card or envelope a profitable investment. You will probably get a higher percentage of returns if you pay the postage, but when you do that, the quality of the inquiries has to be taken into consideration; therefore I say again—to be on the safe side, *make a test.*

Are Postscripts Good or Bad?

In routine correspondence, I agree with Lawrence Lockley, author of "Principles of Effective Letter Writing," that they should be unnecessary.

In sales letters, on the other hand, they can be used with telling effect. Frequently letters are scanned hurriedly, not digested carefully as we intended and hoped when we wrote them. If there is a postscript, however, it may serve to arouse enough interest so that the reader will go back and give the letter another chance. Thus, a skillfully worded postscript *might* mean the difference between success and failure. Now don't go and put one on every letter. Use the postscript as you would any of the many other tools and tricks of letter writing —only when it seems to fit in with the scheme of things.

Here are some P.S.'s that were effectively used:

P.S. If you send off your six months' or year's subscription by return mail, you may deduct the $3 already paid, making the price only $27 for six months or $47 for a full year.

* * *

P.S. Housewives tell us that a glass of milk during the morning and again in the afternoon makes a lot of difference in the way they feel at night.

* * *

P.S. You've probably spent enough money on moth preventatives alone to pay the small service fee for Elite "Clothes Parking."

* * *

P.S. For super mileage, ask to see the amazing new Pennsylvania RX, the tire with feather-bed resiliency, compression tread, noiseless riding, and permanent white walls.

* * *

P.S. It'll soon be time to have your heater cleaned. *We'll do it for you for only* $4.40.

* * *

P.S. We still say that our prices are no higher than you'd pay for a good ready-made.

How Should Letters Be Signed?

A letter should be signed with an individual signature, if practical, otherwise with a facsimile signature that *looks* like an individual signature. The more the letter resembles an individually typewritten letter, the more necessary it is to carry out the illusion of a personal letter by an actual signature or clever machine reproduction. Real progress has been made in the past few years in signature cuts for the multigraph, and those being turned out now are giving excellent results.

In a multigraphed, filled-in letter, the signature should likewise be as personal looking as possible, not for the purpose of deception, but to make the letter look more important and more interesting. The appearance of a letter and the way it is individualized to look like a worth-while message have a lot to do with the prospect's decision as to whether to read the letter and see what it's all about or toss it aside and go on to the next.

How about Enclosures?

Many times the subject of a letter is such that, properly to convey data concerning the product or proposition, it is necessary to resort to an enclosure. Usually, this takes the form of a small booklet or folder, sometimes a single-sheet circular. The enclosure is frequently an important factor in the success of the letter, particularly when it relieves the letter of the necessity for giving technical details, prices, sizes, and similar information.

Such literature, while used to supplement the letter, should be able to stand on its own feet when separated from it. Letters are often thrown away and the enclosure kept for future reference.

When it is being enclosed, the folder, or "stuffer," as it is sometimes called, should be so placed in the fold of the letter that it comes out with it. If it is put in the envelope as a separate piece, the folder might easily be left behind unnoticed.

One other point about enclosures—don't have too many of them. "The more the merrier" doesn't apply to the pieces that go into an envelope. As you divide attention, you lessen interest. A good enclosure will help the letter put across its message. Too many enclosures may ruin everything.

When Is the Best Time to Mail?

The best days for a prospect to receive mail are Tuesdays, Wednesdays, and Thursdays. Friday isn't quite so good, but it is better than Monday or Saturday. Monday, because of the holiday preceding it, is usually a busy day for most people, and therefore on that day they are less apt to consider propositions received through the mail.

Saturday is at least a half holiday, and many take the entire day off even in winter. In any event, it too is a busy day and therefore a poor one on which to attempt to sell by mail.

It shouldn't be necessary to point out that Christmas, New Year's, and other national holidays are good days to stay away from when it comes to mailing *order-* or *inquiry*-seeking material. Give such times of the year a wide berth.

CHAPTER ELEVEN

On Testing

Before the Letter Goes Out

Do you remember, some years back, when your mother used to give you a very careful "once-over" before sending you off to school? Neck and ears clean? Hands and face washed? Hair combed? Clothes in order? Have you got your books?

Well, it's that kind of "once-over" that is meant by *testing before the letter goes out.* How about *its* neck and ears? Rest easy, I won't carry the analogy any farther. However, there are just as many questions you must ask about the letter you have prepared. In an earlier chapter, I suggested that you read it aloud and see how it sounds. That is a mighty good test and one that will uncover many weak spots. But there are a lot of other things to take into consideration before the letter goes out.

How does it *look* when set up on your letterhead all ready to go? Impressive? Interesting? Attractive? Important? Personal?

Is it addressed to the *right person?* Writing to the purchasing agent, when the plant superintendent is really the man, will keep returns down to a minimum.

Are you using an up-to-date list? Are you reasonably sure that the names on it are those of people who *need* and should *want* what you have to offer and can *afford* to buy it?

Is it going out at the *right time?* Monday and Saturday are usually poor days for your letter to arrive. Tuesday is the best day, Wednesday the next, Thursday and Friday after that. Also how about the *time of year?*

The opening paragraph—does it act like a stop signal? Is it interest-creating? Does it make you want to read more?

Is your proposition a good one? Would *you* be interested in it if you were "on the other side of the fence"?

Have you told about it convincingly? Has your story "believability"? Does it sound sincere? Have you given the prospect a motive for doing what you want him to do?

Did you make the right kind of bid for action? Did you give a *reason* for acting? Have you made it easy and convenient for the prospect or customer to reply?

Have you followed the letter formula and adhered to its requirements? It's easy to check up and find out. If you are using enclosures of any kind, are they being put into the envelopes in such a way that they are sure to come out with the letter?

Finally, have you given your letter to someone else to read in order to get an outside slant on your efforts?

A thorough analysis of all the various elements that can influence the success or failure of your letter will prove a really worth-while investment.

Testing after the Letter Goes Out

No, it isn't too late to test after your letter has gone, that is, if your mailing is deliberately sent out as a test. If you "shoot the whole works" and take a chance, it's too late then, of course, but certainly you wouldn't do that if it were at all practicable to make some profitable experiments first.

The average portion of a list to be tested is around 10 per cent. If the ultimate mailing is to 50,000 names, for instance, it would be decidedly in order to use 5,000 of them as laboratory "guinea pigs." Approximately the same percentage of inquiries or orders that is received by the test mailing will be received by the big mailing, all factors being equal.

If you use only the best names for your test, your general mailing will naturally show a smaller percentage. Let the test list be a fair cross section of the whole. If you test at a good time of the month or year and send out the general mailing at an unfavorable time, your results will not be an accurate measuring stick for your letter.

Such observations may be elementary, but they are good points to remember. Sometimes the elementary facts of life are the ones we forget first.

The test itself will vary with the circumstances. In some cases, when the mailing consists of a letter, folder, and return card, it is necessary to write three or more letters, three or more folders, and three or more return cards, and send them out in different combinations. Letter No. 1 with folder No. 2 and card No. 3. Letter No. 2 with folder No. 3 and card No. 1. Letter No. 3 with folder No. 1 and card No. 2.

When you are through, an analysis of returns will show you which is the best letter, which the best folder, and which the best card. A general mailing, using the best of each, should and usually does produce a percentage in excess of that obtained by any of the test mailings. This method of testing is employed by one of the largest mail-selling houses in the country.

In other cases, it is important to test the various elements that make up the letter itself—the opening paragraph, closing paragraph, type of processing (typewriting, multigraphing, printing, etc.), signature, etc. The purpose here, of course, is to find out the relative importance *on results* of each part of the letter.

The way to do it is to send the original letter out to one list, to another section of the list the same letter in every respect except for the opening paragraph, to another similar group the same letter with a different close, etc. When the returns are analyzed, it is a comparatively easy matter to see what combination of elements should be used in the general mailing.

Such testing requires patience and isn't always practical, but it can pay big dividends.

A third method of testing is the simplest of all. You merely send out your letter to a cross section of the list and check results. If they aren't satisfactory based on past experience, you try another appeal and keep trying until you feel that you have exhausted the possibilities—and even then you keep trying.

Testing, from the standpoint of a company selling by mail to consumers, should stay within comparatively narrow limits —keeping these basic principles in mind.

Test to a list large enough for the result to mean something. A thousand names on each side of a preliminary test is just about the minimum. And if your list is 20,000 to 25,000 names or more, a better quantity would be 2,000 to 2,500. Testing a few hundred names doesn't give the law of averages a chance to work.

Test fundamentals. Let somebody else test the *details.* The most important tests for most advertisers looking for orders are of copy, offers, and lists. For those after inquiries, with only one basic list to work on, the testing will generally be of the copy or sales message in various direct mail "packages," *i.e.,* letter, folder, and reply card vs. letter and reply card vs. letter-folder and reply card vs. self-mailer with reply card attached, etc.

Test one thing at a time! Suppose you send half the test list a letter, folder, and reply card and the other half a self-mailer, with the two halves of the list going into different states. Actually then, you're testing *two* variables: one form of direct mail vs. another and one group of states vs. another group. When the results come in, you've learned practically nothing. Mail at the same time, to every other name on the list, with only one factor different; when you get through, the chances are you'll have a helpful comparison to guide you in the future.

What Kind of Returns to Expect?

Obviously there could be no specific answer to this question. The number of orders or inquiries you receive depends on many things—the worth-whileness of the product, the acceptability of the proposition, the believability of the story, the quality of the list, etc. You can see why it is impossible to *predict* with any degree of accuracy what any given mailing will do.

You will know for sure what returns to expect about two weeks after a test mailing has gone out. Before that you can only guess, although with experience you can quite easily arrive at a *reasonable expectation*.

More important is learning how to measure the effectiveness of sales letters after the returns are all in. It is essential that you know how to tell, accurately, whether or not your investment in printed salesmanship is paying satisfactory dividends.

The fact is, you can tell to the penny, in some cases, how much you are getting back for each dollar spent in sales letters. In others, you can't measure the effectiveness quite so accurately but you can at least determine whether your program is accomplishing its objective. To be specific, we'll have to divide the general term SALES LETTERS into a number of different categories:

1. Letters to get *orders*
2. Letters to get *inquiries*

3. Letters to *pave the way for salesmen*
4. Letters to *bring people into a store, showroom, or service station.*

There are many other functions of sales letters, of course, but these four will suffice for this discussion. Let's talk about each from the standpoint of result measurement.

No. 1. *Letters to get orders.* This one is easy. When you use letters to get orders, you either get a profitable percentage or you don't and it's simply a matter of using arithmetic to find out. Here's an example: Let's say a mailing costs $50 a thousand to send out. You mail 10,000 for a total cost of $500. Suppose your unit of sale is $6.50; your cost for the product in the mail, $1.50. That makes the margin of profit on each order $5. Your break-even point therefore is 1 per cent, for 1 per cent of 10,000 is 100 orders and 100 orders times $5 profit on each is $500, which is exactly what the mailing cost you. Thus, if you receive better than 1 per cent, you make money. If you receive *less*, you lose money.

No. 2. *Letters to get inquiries* are almost as easy to measure. You send out a quantity of letters or other type of direct mail and in due course receive back a percentage of inquiry cards. Suppose the mailing is to 10,000. Suppose 5 per cent, or 500 cards, come back. That is your first measurement, but it is useful only for the purposes of comparison with similar efforts to the same list. Whether 5 per cent will prove a *profitable* percentage of return is still to be determined. You go after the 500 leads or inquiries either by mail or with salesmen. The percentage of these which are turned into orders is the important thing, and more important still is the *value* of the orders you close in relation to what they cost you. So let's do some more hypothetical arithmetic. If the original mailing to 10,000 cost $50 per thousand, or $500 total, the 500 inquiries cost you $1 each. Suppose you convert 20 per cent of the inquiries into orders. The 100 orders would then have cost you $5 each, plus the sales or mail cost incurred in following up the inquiries. Whether that is profitable or not depends on the unit of sale, the profit on each sale, and the potential repeat business.

No. 3. *Letters to pave the way for salesmen.* This job of measurement isn't so easy and cannot be anywhere near so accurate. To make the job of selling easier, let's suppose you send out three letters to a given territory in advance of calls by your salesmen. Regardless of how well or how poorly your salesmen make out when they go into that territory, you won't know, of course, to what extent the prospects bought as the direct or indirect result of the direct-mail material they received. The measuring stick used in such cases is COMPARISON. Take a group of salesmen and give them complete direct-mail support. Take another group in a similar territory and give them no direct-mail support whatever. Compare the final results, the amount of business done in each case, the extent of sales resistance encountered, the time it took to complete the sales, the attitude of the salesmen themselves. You will then have a pretty definite idea of how helpful and even how profitable your sales letters were. So even in this situation you have a fairly accurate means of measuring the effectiveness of your letters. My prediction is that, in 90 per cent of the cases where scientifically prepared sales letters are used for this purpose, the result will more than justify the cost.

No. 4. *Letters to bring people into a store, showroom, or service station.* Here again, the job of measurement isn't 100 per cent accurate but it can be done very satisfactorily. This type of advertising will generally fall into one of two classes:

   a. Letters about specific products or services
   b. Letters to build good will and preference

a. When you advertise a specific product, a group of products, or a service of some kind, there is seldom any difficulty in determining whether or not the advertising was productive. The store or individual service station will, of course, know how many pieces were mailed, how much they cost, how many sales resulted, and the total profit that resulted. On the basis of straight arithmetic, the campaign will be profitable or unprofitable.

b. When you use letters to build good will, to create a preference for a particular store or service station, to invite people to come in on the strength of more or less general claims, then the job of measurement becomes more difficult. To check the results, we again resort to COMPARISON. A manufacturer, for instance, sends a sales-letter campaign to *half* the prospects in the vicinity of a dealer's store or service station. To the other half he sends nothing. After the advertising has had time to work, an analysis of results is made to determine *how much* more business was done with the prospects who had been circularized. It is then easy enough to figure out whether it produced enough more business to justify the effort. In most cases you'll find that it has.

Results Varying from 1 to 81 per cent

Following is a group of letters, all good, that produced results as far apart as the Poles. The reason, of course, is obvious —*the objectives were different*. Those designed to bring back orders were lucky to get somewhere around 1 per cent.

Note. There are many instances of higher percentages from letters seeking direct orders, some as high as 8 and 10 per cent. It depends largely on the unit of sale. The lower the price the higher the percentage you will probably receive, but it doesn't follow that it will be a *profitable* percentage.

The highest producer in this group pulled in responses

from 81 per cent of the people who received it, but as you will see, the high returns were greatly influenced by the fact that it offered something of value for nothing. So you see the *objective* is a very big factor.

Letter No. 1. This letter has been mailed in various forms but basically the same to over a million names at a cost of over $100,000. It consistently produced around 1 per cent.

A NEW IDEA—and we *guarantee* you'll like it

This letter is about a new kind of business magazine, different from any you've ever read. It is available only through subscription, not on newsstands.

Here is why I feel so confident you *will* like it—

KIPLINGER MAGAZINE brings you each month 48 pages of helpful, profitable, enjoyable and stimulating material. It's all "meat"—no padding. Every word is a working word.

It contains no advertising and never will. *We have literally no one to please but YOU.* Our editors have a free hand—no restrictions—no sacred cows. Their sole aim is to keep you ahead in your thinking, make it easier for you to keep up with these fast-changing times.

Briefly, here's what KIPLINGER MAGAZINE will do for you—

It will help you do your job better, by telling you what others are doing. It will help you look farther ahead, by giving you dependable forecasts of the future. It will help you plan more wisely, by giving you essential facts, experiences and worth-while opinions. It will entertain and stimulate you as no other business magazine you have ever read.

All articles in KIPLINGER MAGAZINE are short, crisp, easy to read. Each month's issue covers as many as 85 different subjects, yet you can read it from beginning to end in a single evening. And the pages are perforated so any article can be quickly removed for filing or passing along to others.

One important reason for the quick acceptance and steady growth of this unusual magazine is its top editor— W. M. Kiplinger—whose weekly Washington Letter has been a Monday morning "must" to American business-men for 25 years. To thousands of executives all over the country, that was reason enough for giving KIPLINGER MAGAZINE a fair trial. *But they renewed their subscrip-tions, many for two years, solely because they liked what they read. And you will, too.*

You're successful today. You want to keep on climbing. That's why I know you're not content with the super-ficial reporting that satisfies the crowd. You want some-thing special *and this new idea in editing is it!*

But you needn't take OUR word for it. Although the yearly subscription rate is $6, you may try KIPLINGER MAGAZINE on an introductory basis—5 months for only $2—and see for yourself what it can do for you.

Fill out the enclosed card and service will start with the issue now going to press.

Cordially,

Letter No. 2. Orders resulting from this letter to a specialized field totaled 245 from a list of 14,220 banks. Sample labels, order form, and a return envelope were enclosed.

In addition, 54 inquiries were received from which came 16 orders, bringing the total return to 261 (1.8 per cent). The orders were for $2,176.67 worth of business, secured at a cost of $784.

MAY WE MAKE A SUGGESTION?

There's no time like the present to check your supply of labels—to make sure you have plenty of those quality FENT-ONAMEL labels that are so much in keeping with the prestige and standing of your bank.

True, the label is a small item but through it, many thousands of people receive a constant reminder of the banking institution of their choice. That's only one reason why so many banks all over the country continue using Fent-Onamel labels, year in and year out.

The colors and clean-cut printing on fine paper add dignity and make good-looking labels for envelopes, statements, calendars, mailing, etc., issued by banks. The gold or platinum tint labels are particularly effective and rich-looking for stocks, bonds and other documents.

FENT-ONAMEL labels are the finest you can buy. We now make them in all sizes, all quantities and up to four colors on gummed or ungummed stock.

From the samples enclosed, you will see a few of the many shapes and sizes already in use—some that may be suitable for your needs. After you have looked them over, insure prompt service by filling in and mailing the convenient order form today.

Sincerely,

Letter No. 3. This letter is a good example of how a very unpretentious-looking and inexpensive letter can pay big dividends.

The *Town Journal Magazine* made a selective mailing to individuals living in towns under 50,000 population, where no previous *Town Journal* mailings had been made.

They sent out 80,397 letters which brought in 1,485 orders,

a return of 1.85 per cent. The total cost of the mailing was $1,640, the orders amounted to $4,095, and the resulting profit was $2,455. Another way of looking at the results—for every 1,000 letters mailed they received a profit of $30.68.

Please keep this letter as your GUARANTEE

—that any time you feel you are not getting a lot more than your money's worth from this offer—

> *your money will be refunded*
> *instantly and without question!*

This letter is also your guarantee that in each issue you will receive:

***Reliable facts and forecasts*

In the Washington letter, "Under the Dome," you get more than fifteen really worth-while TIPS—complete advance information—with accurate predictions to help you plan more wisely, more safely for the future.

***The "Looking Ahead" letter*

Business and professional men in communities similar to yours tell us this forecast letter is what they have always wanted. It's a full-page preview of what's coming that will affect business and your personal life.

***Dependable analyses of all the news*

You receive pages of news about what's happening all over the world as well as the Washington and nation-wide news. And, most important—you get an *explanation of what it all means to you.*

Yes, you receive all this and a lot more in every issue of the new, bigger and better *Town Journal.* And, the best part of it is—you can have it mailed to your home for a full year (26 BIG ISSUES) for only $2. Or, you can save a dollar by taking advantage of the Extra Value Special: 2 years (52 BIG ISSUES) for only $3—which is less than 3¢ a week!

Think of it—for less than 3¢ a week *Town Journal* will keep you up on things of importance. And, when you talk about them to your business associates, friends and neighbors, you will know that you speak with authority. What's more—the two Washington forecast letters in every issue will give you predictions that might easily be worth many times the price of *Town Journal* for a lifetime.

And, remember—at any time—for any reason, or for no reason—you can have a cash refund of the unused part of your subscription.

Because you can't possibly lose—take advantage of this amazing offer NOW. Your name and address are already printed on the enclosed order form. All you need to do is:

—indicate your choice of the low rates

—and attach your remittance.

Then mail it TODAY in the enclosed, addressed envelope.

Cordially,

P.S. Should dollar bills be more convenient to send than check or money order—we'll accept the risk.

Letter No. 4. This letter was mailed by the *Farm Journal* to 3,587,507 rural route and star route boxholders over a period of three months. It was the sixth mailing that had been made to these same boxholders in five years to get subscriptions to the *Farm Journal*.

The letter brought in a total return of 88,611 orders, or 2.47 per cent. The total profit on the mailing, $11,514.

In considering results from letters of this kind, it must be remembered that many of these new customers will renew their subscriptions year after year. That, of course, will add materially to the return on the original investment.

IF YOU DON'T READ THIS LETTER NOW,
YOU WILL WONDER ALL DAY WHAT IT SAYS.

It will take you only a minute to sit down and read this letter right now. And—you'll be glad you did because it brings you the biggest bargain in America.

What's more—when you take advantage of this amazing bargain, you are guaranteed that you can have a cash refund—at any time—for any reason or for no reason.

That's fair enough, isn't it?

Now, here is what you and your family will receive every month:

For Women

New recipes that are quick and easy to prepare. And —when you put them on the table you'll hear, "Umm— that's good, Mother."

Every month you will receive up-to-date fashions... complete with patterns.

Ideas on decorating—ways to give rooms a new look— how to do it easily and economically—by yourself if you wish.

Hints on how to save time and toil with your housework. Ideas that other women have used and found helpful. You know, for example—when hanging the wash, pin one pillow case with open end up. When taking dry wash down, put all small pieces into this pillow case. It saves time when sprinkling.

For Men

Every month you'll get a full page of valuable, farmborn ideas that you can put to work on your farm. Pictures and diagrams that show you how to make handy, labor-saving devices that do the job better, easier and quicker.

News about new money-making crops, new farm machinery, buildings and proven ways of cutting down production costs.

Suggestions on when to buy, when to sell, what to feed and what to plant. These are dependable facts and accurate forecasts based on last-minute telegraphed reports from all over the country. Farmers tell us and records prove that four out of every five predictions *make them money*. In addition, your entire family will enjoy the good, clean fiction and jokes. Your children will like the separate departments for boys and girls. And, you receive all this—not just one time, but every month in FARM JOURNAL and FARMER'S WIFE.

Now—here is a pleasant surprise—you can have 12 Big Issues—every one of them filled with new, different, valuable information—for only 50¢. Or, you get 24 Big Issues (2 Years) for only a dollar. And, here's the greatest bargain of all—5 *full years (60 Big Issues) for only $2.*

THINK OF THIS—there is only one magazine in America (no other farm magazine) with as many mail subscribers as FARM JOURNAL and FARMER'S WIFE. It is one of the Nation's largest and best magazines. Yet, you get every issue for an entire year for less than the price of a single copy of many magazines. And, the editors have big plans for every issue this year. The February and March issues are already scheduled for 180 pages or more! That's why we say—you get so much for so little.

Is it any wonder that FARM JOURNAL is read in more homes than any other farm magazine? After 70 years of pleasant relationships with farmers, more than 2,650,000 satisfied families now read every issue. And, every day hundreds of letters come in telling us FARM JOURNAL is worth many times the low purchase price. One received today said: "I don't understand how you can publish such a valuable magazine at so low a cost. It's getting better every month." You will like it, too.

To get every issue, print your name, route number and post office on the MONEY-BACK GUARANTEE card. Fold in two quarters, stamps, 50¢, dollar bills, check or money order. Whatever you send—*we'll take the risk*. Why not mail the card in the already addressed envelope right now. You can't possibly lose because you can have a cash refund of the unused part of your subscription any time you want it.

Cordially,

P.S. Here's a friendly tip—increased costs may force us to raise the low price of FARM JOURNAL, as other magazines already have. If you are a subscriber, protect yourself by extending your subscription NOW—before it expires. (New subscribers—protect yourself by taking advantage of the 5-YEAR BARGAIN OFFER—just slightly over 3¢ a copy!)

Letter No. 5. This was No. 1 in a series sent to inquiries from publication advertising about Chinchilla rabbits. Approximately 15,000 of these letters were sent out over a period of six months in reply to such requests, and the orders resulting amounted in number to about 400, in percentage to 2.7, in dollars to about $20,000. A booklet, order form, and reply envelope accompanied the letter. Another 400 sales resulted from the follow-up letters.

HERE'S THE INFORMATION YOU REQUESTED
ABOUT THIS AMAZING ENTERPRISE

Dear Friend:

You are in line for participation in one of America's

most promising industries. . . . You can establish a profitable branch "factory" right in your own backyard. With no experience or training, with very little capital, only a small part of your time and no interference with your regular job or business, you can soon be a full-fledged breeder of Chin-Chin Giant Chinchillas, King of Rabbits and largest money maker of them all.

Here's a business where you will produce highly profitable, *essential products*. The delicious meat so sorely needed now and in the years ahead, and the gorgeous furs so sought after by fashionable women everywhere at all times.

Chin-Chins produce more *meat* in a shorter period of time than other rabbits. Chin-Chins also produce the most gorgeous, most durable, and most valuable of all rabbit *furs* in America. In addition, they produce *leather, felt, glue, lab-stock, vaccines,* etc. Chin-Chin Giant Chinchillas have been painstakingly developed to be the *most prolific* of all rabbits.

All this adds up to an opportunity for you to make almost unbelievable profits. Here is a chance to set up a "factory" that will practically run itself—your own business with no production tie-ups, no labor problems, and no worries about marketing your products.

Chin-Chin fur is in *tremendous demand* now. About two-thirds of the furs used in America are rabbit furs! Over 200,000,000 rabbit furs are used in this country each year. Chin-Chin furs are the most valuable of all because they so closely resemble the most fabulous of all furs— that of the delicate Chinchilla Lanigera—and yet Chin-Chin fur wears years longer.

Chin-Chin meat can be produced *cheaper* than other meat. Government figures prove that rabbits produce more pounds of meat per pound of feed than any other kind of domestic animal. Chin-Chin Giant Chinchillas put on more weight in a shorter period of time than other rabbits.

Because they are almost universally recognized as the *finest commercial rabbits known,* Chin-Chin *breeding stock* is in tremendous demand. Even though we are by far the largest producers of these rabbits in America, we cannot possibly fill the ever-increasing demand for breeders.

To supplement present sources of supply for Chin-Chin breeding stock, a great MANY MORE NEW BREEDERS are urgently needed, so that this RAPIDLY INCREASING DEMAND can be met by an EVER-INCREASING SUPPLY of Chin-Chins.

To this end . . . we invite you to enter this highly interesting and profitable business . . . which you can do on a total capital outlay of less than $75 for Chin-Chins and Hutches (arranged on easy payments if you prefer).

Many of our customers have consistently made profits of up to 1,000% on their investment! Do you know of any other business which will produce such a high profit for such a small investment?

Would you be interested in making such a profit? OF COURSE YOU WOULD! . . . But first, naturally enough, you want to be sure that it CAN be done and HAS been done, over and over again. Take this opportunity to PROVE it to YOUR OWN SATISFACTION by examining the facts and figures and the experiences of others.

From a small beginning, with a Trio of two Chin-Chin does and one buck . . . you can soon be raising many, many Chin-Chins yearly . . . thus converting your spare-time "hobby" into a full-time, high-profit business . . .

selling your production to us or to others for breeding stock ... or doing a big-scale commercial rabbit business in the production and sale of fur pelts and meat.

More about this interesting, highly profitable industry is told in the illustrated folder accompanying this letter. Read it over carefully. You'll learn immediately why raising Chin-Chins—Aristocrats of Rabbitdom—is so much *more profitable* and *easier* than raising other rabbits, poultry, or any other kind of livestock.

Chin-Chins can be successfully raised in the hottest and coldest climates encountered in North America ... no heat or air-conditioning is ever needed.

Note the small amount of time and attention that Chin-Chins require, particularly when housed in our ABC Hutches. Raising Chin-Chins offers a better, brighter, more prosperous future to anyone who has grown tired of salaried servitude and the monotony of uninteresting, small pay job in office, shop, or store, and who is hungering for personal and financial independence.

Note the letters from satisfied customers who are making money with Chin-Chins now. Here's how one of our Florida customers expressed it:

"Just 18 months ago I received my first Chin-Chins. At that time I had 1,500 chickens, two helpers and all the headaches that go with poultry. Today I have no hens, no helpers, no headaches, and profits from my rabbits are about five times what they were on poultry, with about one-third the expense and it is really a pleasure to work with these Chins— They are so gentle and easy to handle."

Living costs are rising—and we don't know how long

we shall be able to maintain our present price levels. But, if you ACT NOW, you can RECEIVE the *benefits* of PRICE INCREASES instead of PAYING THEM.

An order form and reply envelope—no postage needed —are enclosed for your convenience. GET YOUR ORDER IN THE MAIL TODAY! You'll be glad you did!

Sincerely,

Letter No. 6. This was one of three letters sent to a list of 10,000 manufacturers to get requests for a booklet about the city of Camden, N.J.

Only those who might be interested in moving to a new location would have any reason for replying, so the percentage return was low—about 3.5 per cent. *But out of the 350 replies, enough resulted in new industries coming to Camden to make the mailings exceedingly worth while.*

Thinking of MOVING or DECENTRALIZING?

If so, there are some fine possibilities in Camden, New Jersey. We have prepared an illustrated booklet giving specific information that we should like very much to send you.

Included are a great many pertinent facts about Camden and Camden County—telling and picturing what we have to offer you in the way of advantages, plus values, proximity to important markets, special features, etc.

As you know, there has been considerable change in the whole method of distribution for many manufacturers. Literally thousands of firms are decentralizing, to get closer to raw materials, save transportation costs and improve their distribution picture. Others are moving to this area to get into better position for export business.

Whatever your particular reason, if you are at all interested in another location, may we send you the story of
Camden, New Jersey?

Just mail the enclosed card and we'll put your copy in
the return mail.

Sincerely,

Letter No. 7. Here is a "trouble-shooter" type of appeal—an
excellent example of a straightforward letter that comes right
out and asks customers why they have not been ordering.

Out of a list of 759 customers, 283 replies *were received, a
return of 37 per cent.* The letter was sent first class with a return envelope enclosed.

The whole mailing cost less than $100, and the result was
extremely satisfactory.

Gentlemen:

Will you do something for me?

All I want is a little information, which you can give
me very quickly. I've always believed in being straightforward so without any beating around the bush, here is
the question I'd like answered—

Why, please, aren't we getting more of your business?

To the best of my knowledge, French's products are as
fine quality, dependable, and fairly priced as any on the
market. The margin of profit we allow dealers is excep-
tionally high (40%).

I suppose every manufacturer has a tendency to think
that everything he does is okay—and that when sales
aren't booming, it's somebody else who's out of step. But
I don't believe that, or I certainly wouldn't be writing
you this way.

To make it easy for you to reply, use the bottom of this
letter, or the reverse side—then mail in the enclosed

stamped envelope. I'll appreciate a very frank answer, with no punches pulled.

Many thanks for your courtesy.

Sincerely,

Mr. Longstreth: The reasons we haven't been giving you more of our business are:

Letters Nos. 8, 9, 10. These three letters prove conclusively that direct mail, properly prepared, *will* be opened and read —even by busy executives. The returns on all three letters were considerably above average, due to the character of the appeal, the skill with which it was made, the type of mailing, and the nature of the offer.

All three letters were designed to secure leads for future business through the effective device of offering something of value for nothing.

The Air Express letter sent out in a test mailing *pulled a return of 34.8 per cent.*

The American Airlines letter pulled 2,080 replies out of a possible 4,000—*a 52 per cent return.*

The Lafayette Radio letter gained added appeal by personalizing its offer. Mailed to 488 executives, *it brought replies from 366, or a return of 81 per cent!*

Dear Mr. Doe:

We are planning to mail to you within the next few days—with no obligation, of course, an especially timely and helpful Handbook on Air Express shipping. To make sure that it reaches the proper executive, will you help us by checking and returning the enclosed card?

Entitled, "How to Ship by Air Express during Wartime," this Handbook gives you complete data on "fastest way" shipping. It supplements, for executive use, the wall chart prepared especially for use in shipping rooms, a copy of which has already been sent to you.

This reference booklet begins by answering the questions most frequently asked right now about Air Express —those relating to *priorities.* When should they be requested—who should apply for them—who grants them —what data is necessary in requesting a priority? Included is a map of the 19 Air Priority Control Regions, with a list of the states and counties in each region—plus the addresses and phone numbers of the Regional Priority Offices.

This information should be especially useful right now —though as you probably know, non-priority shipments are accepted on a space available basis and are carried subject to preferences of priority. Nevertheless, when the nature of a shipment justifies it, *a priority will be granted, and should be requested.*

Besides details of the priority set-up, all of the other basic information on Air Express is here too. For example, the Handbook tells you what things can go by air— the few exceptions that cannot. It gives the story on maximum package size and weight and includes a convenient table of rates for typical shipments. And it provides on the back cover, for easy reference, a map of the Air Express System—where you can find the approximate flying time between any two airport cities in America.

The Handbook offers many suggestions you will find it helpful to follow and should prove of real value in providing immediate answers to any questions you may have on Air Express shipping. Just check the correctness of name and address on the postage-paid card enclosed, and send it back to us. We'll mail your copy as soon as it comes off the press—without cost or obligation.

Very truly yours,

Dear Mr. Gerard:

We are currently publishing a book on modern air transportation which we believe will be read with exceptional interest by a great many people.

Because of this, we are making arrangements to distribute complimentary copies on request, and take this opportunity of inquiring whether you would like to have a copy sent to you upon publication. If so, please let us know by sending the request card attached to this letter.

This book might almost be called the History and Progress of American Transport Aviation—because it pictures so many of the developments which have made Air Transportation one of the country's big industries.

It presents a variety of interesting facts and explanations about airline operation which many people are not familiar with. For example, why Airliners carry thousands of dollars in equipment which is never used—how flight officers are trained—how the radio beam and radio communications work—how today's amazingly dependable weather forecasting is carried on. Included are over 100 photographs and color illustrations in 24 magazine-size pages of text, with answers to many aviation questions which are frequently asked and not always very accurately answered.

We are publishing this book after 12 years of service as the country's largest airline, to acquaint the public more fully with the background and development of air transport in general and of American Airlines in particular—and to give a clear picture of the standards and methods that have made American transport aviation the finest in the world.

In order to have a copy sent to you, please make use of the card enclosed—but may we ask your cooperation in returning it promptly, since it will help us greatly to receive as many requests as possible now, while the book is still in publication.

Yours sincerely,

Dear Mr. Doe:

We are planning to send you within the next few days —and without cost or obligation—a complimentary copy of the new Radio's Master Encyclopedia, 9th Edition, with your name gold-stamped on the cover. However, before we send it, and to make sure we have your name spelled correctly, will you help us by checking and returning the enclosed card?

You are probably already familiar with this unusually comprehensive catalog of radio parts and equipment. For years radio men have known it as the standard reference book, buying guide and encyclopedia in the radio and electronic field. Compiled with the cooperation of the Radio Manufacturer's Group, it has been approved by this group as the industry's official source book.

In its over 800 pages this Master Encyclopedia contains descriptions, illustrations and specifications of thousands of items such as radio parts and electronic equipment. And a complete reference index, by type of item and manufacturer, enables you to find any part quickly and easily.

Ordinarily this encyclopedia sells for $2.50. However, because of its value and importance, we have secured a limited number of copies for complimentary distribution to key executives, like yourself, who are interested in the type of material it contains.

We'll be glad to send your copy of this helpful and informative encyclopedia, with your name gold-stamped on the cover—without cost or obligation. But so that we may be sure that your name will be printed correctly on the cover, will you please check the enclosed card and return it to us? The card requires no postage—just check it and drop it in the mail.

Very truly yours,

Measuring Stick for Sales Letters

You're planning to send out a *sales* letter to a group of prospects and you want *results*. You have the copy for such a letter before you and are wondering whether it's any good or not. Well, here's a way to find out. Analyze it with the help of this check list. Be honest and you'll quickly highlight weaknesses in the letter if any exist.

☐ Does ☐ Does not follow the sales-letter formula—interest, desire, conviction, action

Opening is ☐ excellent ☐ good ☐ uninteresting ☐ weak ☐ complicated

☐ Benefits from use of product or service brought in very effectively

☐ Doesn't mention benefits—fails to create desire

☐ Does a complete selling job ☐ Doesn't sell enough—lacks conviction

☐ Smooth reading—well constructed ☐ Doesn't hang together—lacks continuity

☐ Closing paragraph—good

☐ Closing paragraph—weak. No adequate bid for action

☐ Too much "We—Our—Us"   ☐ Wordy and involved

☐ Lacks sincerity

☐ Too many hackneyed and stereotyped words and expressions

CHAPTER TWELVE

Letter Don'ts

Don't address your letter to a company if you can possibly get the name of the proper individual. For one thing, more of your letters will get to their ultimate destination, *i.e.,* the person in the company most interested; for another, you can make your letter more personal.

Don't use mouse gray as a color for your letterhead or return envelope. Yellow, buff, or cherry will stand out much better.

Don't send out letters *"any old time."* Select the time for your mailing carefully and wisely, taking into consideration all the various factors.

Don't use a small, insignificant order blank. Not giving a prospect enough space in which to write usually makes him mad. And speaking of order blanks, it is said that a novelty form works better than a commonplace one.

Don't have your letter, order blank, and return envelope all the same color. Contrasting colors for some reason bring back more orders.

Don't insist on the prospect's printing his name and address. Some people don't like to print, and this gives them a chance to put off replying.

Don't let your prospect hesitate about doing what you want him to do. Make your request for action sound urgent!

Don't use a flimsy return envelope. A lot of people are reluctant to send money through the mails anyway.

Don't make the mistake of thinking that details aren't important. The little things about a letter put together constitute the letter itself, and every one of them, like the separate parts of an automobile, is essential to proper functioning.

Don't forget to study, learn by heart, and follow closely the letter formula.

CHAPTER THIRTEEN

Illustrated Letters

There are certain situations wherein the plain all-type letter isn't strong enough, by itself, to carry the load.

In such instances there are two generally accepted solutions. One is to enclose with the letter a folder, circular, or stuffer of some kind and use that for the pictorial and descriptive part of the story.

The other and many times preferable way is use of the illustrated letter, which has several advantages over its competitor, the stuffer. It can't become separated from the letter. It can't be forgotten in the mailing process, as can the separate enclosure, and it isn't so easily misplaced or lost in filing.

Once you've decided that the message calls for illustration and display, the next step is to decide which type of illustrated letter to adopt as the vehicle.

You can inject illustration at the top, bottom, side, or back of your regular letterhead, whether 8½ by 11, Monarch, or baronial size.

You can put a flap at the top or side of your present letterhead and use that for pictures and detailed information.

You can take a standard 8½-by-11 sheet, for instance, fold it once sideways to 6½ by 8½, have your letter in the inside 6½-by-8½ space and use the other space, two sides, for pictures and copy; folded once more, it will fit into an envelope 7 by 4½.

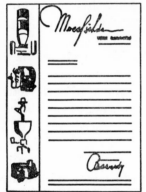

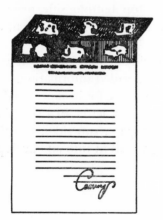

You can take a somewhat larger sheet, say 17 by 8½, fold it down to 8½ by 11 with the 6-inch flap extending from the top. That, counting both sides, will give you 102 square inches of space for the printed section. You can do a lot of explaining and illustrating in an area like that.

Or, you can use the regular four-page letter, 17 by 11, folding to 8½ by 11, with the letter on page one, copy and illustrations on pages two and three, and whatever you want or nothing on page four. Frequently the back page of a four-page letter is left blank so that, when it is folded to go in a number 9 or 10 envelope, no printing meets the eye to lead the prospect to begin reading at the wrong place.

This four-page letter can, of course, be in any size, although the usual sizes of the flat sheets are 17 by 11, folding to 8½ by 11; 15½ by 10½, folding to 7¾ by 10½; and 8½ by 11, folding to 5½ by 8½. All of these may be cut economically out of the standard grades of paper.

Incidentally, there is a wide selection when it comes to choosing the stock for the job. You can use a bond; you can select from dozens of antiques and offset papers and, by using offset lithography, reproduce any kind of illustration, including photographs and wash drawings. You can get papers that are bond on one side for your letter and coated on the other side for your printed matter and cuts; others are colored and coated on both sides, but in different colors.

Certainly there is no excuse for not finding a vehicle for your message that exactly suits it, one that is appropriate from every standpoint.

The size, shape, and color scheme naturally will depend on the character of the product, the kind of proposition, and the type of prospect. The proper selection is a challenge to your skill and judgment and should be made only after an extremely careful study of all the elements involved.

CHAPTER FOURTEEN *Letter Uses*

H ow many different ways do *you* use letters?

There may be some that haven't occurred to you—some that might be the means of increasing your sales volume.

Generally speaking, letters are used to buy and sell merchandise, solicit inquiries, collect accounts, adjust complaints, revive old business, increase good will, stimulate salesmen, build mailing lists, and educate employees. There are a lot of other things, however, that the business letter can do for you, and you should at least know what they are.

More specifically, then, letters can find out why an order wasn't forthcoming after you had so promptly answered an inquiry, discover the opinion of dealers and consumers of your product or service, follow up or prepare the way for a salesman's call, gather credit information, determine the reason for weakness in any given territory, eliminate friction between dealers or salesmen, extend or refuse credit, find new employees, sell dealers on the idea of cooperating, and develop new uses or new markets for your product. There are countless other useful and valuable functions.

When one gets into the subject of letters, there are two phases to be considered—how to improve the type of letters you now use and how to extend the scope of your letter activities to make your stationery more productive. Think it over. Are you supporting your salesmen as you should? Are you giving your dealers all the cooperation you might? Are you covering all the avenues for possible business that can be covered profitably? Do your stenographers and typists have lists and form letters that they can be writing whenever they catch up with their regular work?

Build an outline of the possibilities for letters in your office, making it, of course, fit the facilities for sending them out. As part of that outline or chart, start an "idea file" for supplying the material for the letters you find you can use. Take six manila folders or envelopes and label them *"Ideas about our product or service," "Ideas about quality, price, and usefulness," "Ideas about materials and methods," "Ideas about business policies," "Ideas about plans and their execution,"* and *"Ideas about work standards or discipline."*

Give various men in your office a list of those subjects and encourage them to keep on the lookout, all the time, for ideas for the idea file. (Incidentally, such a file would be of inestimable value in your advertising work too.) In this way you will be stimulating new ideas and new ways in which to use them.

If at the same time you are constantly improving *all* letters from the standpoint of friendliness, conciseness, tone, etc., you can't help but step up the efficiency of your correspondence department by a very sizable percentage.

CHAPTER FIFTEEN

Dictated Letters

We come now to everyday, routine correspondence—the dozens and, in many offices, hundreds of letters that are dictated every day. These letters are a tremendous factor in the building (or tearing down) of sales and good will. If there is any doubt in your mind about the importance of this subject, give a thought to the amount of money spent annually by the average-size company in the answering of its routine mail.

Figuring the dictator's time, stenographer's time, filing, stationery, postage, etc., the cost of a dictated letter today ranges from a dollar to two dollars—an average of $1.50 a letter. There are approximately 300 working days in the year. To find the approximate annual cost of your correspondence, therefore, multiply the number of letters sent out each day by 300 and then by $1.50.

For example:

25	letters a day cost	$ 11,250	a year
50	letters a day cost	22,500	a year
75	letters a day cost	33,750	a year
100	letters a day cost	45,000	a year
150	letters a day cost	67,500	a year
200	letters a day cost	90,000	a year
250	letters a day cost	112,500	a year
300	letters a day cost	135,000	a year
350	letters a day cost	157,500	a year

Correspondence is one of the most important forms of advertising. It makes friends—or breaks them. It builds up—or tears down. It creates the right impression of your company —or the wrong one.

For that reason *every letter, regardless of its purpose, should be a sales letter—whether it goes to one person or many—whether dictated or painstakingly composed.* More firms are realizing this every day, and the tendency is decidedly in the direction of friendlier and more "modern" letters.

Down through the ages has come a certain feeling of casualness toward the dictated letter. The procedure many times is to call in a stenographer. "Miss So-and-so, take a letter...."

Smith, Jones and Smith
So-and-so St.
New York, New York
Gentlemen:

We beg to acknowledge your inquiry of even date and can quote you $6.00 per dozen, f.o.b. our platform. Terms 2%—10 days, net—60.

Trusting this is the information you desire, and thanking you for past favors, we remain,

That goes on hour after hour, almost mechanically, and certainly without the slightest thought for the *effect* of these letters on those who ultimately receive them. The all-consuming idea is to get through with the day's dictation so as to make room for "more important work"—as if there *was any* more important than the molding of favorable opinion in the minds of customers and prospects.

Witness the following "horrible example," the first paragraph of a letter actually sent out by one of the largest department stores in the country.

Noting your remarks on the back of the statement of your July purchases in reference to a rug you sent to us to be cleaned which you advise us one of the rugs have been delivered to you which when cleaned the color ran. (It doesn't even make sense, does it?)

The routine letters that go out of your office every day—letters answering inquiries, adjusting complaints, acknowledging orders, asking for money, etc.—are losing a golden opportunity if they don't do *more* than they set out to do.

It might be the "job" of a letter to acknowledge an order. It should do more than that. Just by the tone, the language, and attitude it adopts, it can unconsciously convey to the mind of your customer or prospect a conviction that yours is a substantial, reliable, friendly company—and that feeling invariably results in increased business.

Three Kinds of Impression

All letters make one of three kinds of impression: *unfavorable* (in that they make you mad, disgusted, sarcastic, discouraged); *colorless* (in that they leave you "cold"); or *favorable* (in that they are completely satisfying. They bring you closer to the writer and to the organization of which the writer is a part. They are friendly, interesting, helpful.) Is there any reason why you shouldn't take advantage of the fact that *all* of your letters can make a *favorable* impression? Such letters cost the same. They generally don't take any longer to dictate or type. They take less time to read and understand. They do two jobs instead of one, in that they properly perform their function, whatever it may be, and in addition they do a good public relations job.

The satisfaction that you as the creator of a good letter can get from being its pappy or mammy is something worth striving for.

A well-written letter pays extra dividends. Not only does it do a better job, make a better impression, get better results— there's a lot of satisfaction in it for the author, too.

You've often done something that gave you a real thrill merely because you knew you had done it well. Maybe it was making something with your hands; it may have been a good speech. But whatever it was, the realization that you had done a good job gave you that "grand and glorious feelin'."

You'll get that same feeling of satisfaction from a well-written letter. A friendlier letter will always give it to you. And by the way, to write friendlier letters, the first thing to do is to feel friendlier as you write.

Some letters are what might be called straight up and down, unfriendly, not actually antagonistic—but *stiff*.

You don't make friends by being *stiff*. If two strangers meet and there is the least bit of yielding or friendliness displayed by either, both of them begin to *warm up*. However, in business letters, we can't be too friendly or we defeat our purpose. We can't be too informal or we might do more harm than good.

But we *can* go part of the way. Depending on the kind of a company yours is, it's up to you to "put on the brakes" at the right point, to decide how far your letters can go in being friendly without going "overboard."

WRONG   RIGHT   WRONG

No matter what your particular function in your present position, consider yourself as one of your company's representatives—in short, a "salesman." You *are* that if in any way you come in contact with your firm's customers or prospects. You can help them decide whether they would like to do business with you or continue doing business with you. You can help or hinder the work of your sales department, supplement or completely nullify the work of your advertising. You can be a marvelous asset to your firm if you just remember one thing: *You*, the things you say and do, your attitude toward your job are as important to the success of your company as the *quality* of the goods or services it sells.

For that reason, you should know something about *sales letters*, even though you may never be called upon to write them.

I want you to know something about sales-letter writing because the objective of every correspondent, whether engaged in sales work or otherwise, should be to make *every* letter a *sales* letter.

If I were to ask you for a definition of a sales letter, I think you would tell me that it is a letter designed to sell something, but you would probably have in mind merchandise, a product of some kind, or some kind of service. The fact is, you have a sales job to do even when you are turning down the request of an applicant for a position. It isn't *essential* that you write a sales letter in a case like that, *but it would help to build good will for your company if you did.*

I should like to impress upon you the fact that you, too, have a selling job to do. Every letter you write, however routine or commonplace its function, can and should create a favorable impression, can and should give the *right idea* of the company sending it out. *It can and should help to build good will.*

Following are some good points to keep in mind.

Point No. 1. Make EVERY Letter a SALES Letter

Now, let me show you how you can make *every* letter a sales letter, regardless of its purpose. There are two ways. One I call the *indirect* way, which is simply saying the same thing in a little friendlier fashion. Thus, indirectly you can do a *public relations* job for your company. Don't forget that hundreds or thousands of people perhaps are influenced by the character of the letters you send out. That's why I want you, first of all, to write *friendlier* letters.

Here is the *colorless* type of letter:

> Your favor of the 20th ult. is at hand, with enclosures as stated. We will do our best to forward the goods promptly and in good order, and will see that your instructions are complied with in every particular.

To illustrate the *indirect* method of making any letter a sales letter, let's say the same thing in a little friendlier way:

> Thank you for your letter of April 20th enclosing the information requested. We shall follow your instructions

in every particular and you can be sure will make shipment of the goods just as quickly as possible.

One way to "unbend" in your letters is to *write as you talk.* I think it safe to say that if you do come a little closer to *writing as you talk* you won't use such expressions as "We are pleased to . . ." In talking with another person you would most likely say "We are very glad to . . ." When you say "We are pleased," you are using words that just don't *"click."* I want you to start using words that *do* "click." Every word and sentence in a letter give a photographic impression of the person or organization sending it out. Some words don't register because they have been used too many times over so many years that they have become virtually meaningless.

Don't Be a Slave to Grammar

In his very excellent book "The Art of Plain Talk," Dr. Rudolf Flesch says, "What is correct grammar? Often it is nothing but rules set up by school teachers to stop language from going where it wants to go."

Now, wait. This isn't going to be a plea for bad English. Certainly our everyday correspondence shouldn't be downright ungrammatical. But too often the dictator, feeling a deeply ingrained sense of obligation to the English language, indulges in faultless prose which is void of any warmth or friendliness.

A good letter writer frequently throws some of the pettier rules of grammar out the window in order to achieve *naturalness,* and to help him better express his own personality. He may use a sentence without a subject, like "Sorry, Mr. Johnson, but we just can't deliver by the tenth." Or he may not use a sentence at all. Like this. Or he may occasionally split an infinitive or end up with a preposition. So *what?* An English professor, measuring it with the yardstick of grammar, might give him a poor mark. But if the customer or prospect *warms up to it,* sees it literally glow with *friendliness and sincerity,* isn't that a more desirable result?

Now, let's talk about the *direct* way of turning a letter into a sales letter. This we do by *adding something to the message* that will have a tendency to bring the person receiving the letter a little "closer" to your company, a little gladder that he bought, or a little more receptive to any new solicitations. The cost of such an addition, both in time and effort, is negligible, yet the dividends in increased good will can be enormous.

Following is the same letter with "something added":

> Thank you for your letter of April 20th enclosing the information requested. We shall follow your instructions in every particular and you can be sure will make shipment of the goods just as quickly as possible.
>
> This particular lot is one of the finest we have ever made and we know you will be well pleased.

So, where it is practical to inject something into the message that will help the letter do a *sales* job, by all means do it.

Assignment. *Take one of your letters and rewrite it two ways* —(*1*) *using the* INDIRECT *way, saying the same thing in a little friendlier fashion, and* (2) *using the* DIRECT *way, by adding something to the answer.*

Point No. 2. Write FRIENDLY Letters

This pointer has to do with *how* to make letters make friends, and I mean all kinds of letters.

First let's keep in mind that in the strict sense of the word, companies as such *can't* read letters. *Individuals* in companies do the reading but lots of times we forget that when we start out a letter with "Gentlemen." You'll write warmer, friendlier letters, if as you dictate you see in your mind's eye a living person across the desk from you. Not a *name,* but a *person.* Flesh and blood. A guy who can be a darn good salesman for *your* company if he gets the right impression from your letters. In future transactions, he can be a real help to you, or a millstone around your neck, depending largely on whether he *likes* you or not. And he *will* like you if you write the right kind of letters—*friendly* letters.

You make friends with people, whether in personal contacts or in correspondence, by being *sympathetic*—sympathetic to their interests, to their problems. *Put yourself in their shoes.* Don't just give information. *Give it wholeheartedly.* And give it with the distinct impression that you are *glad* to be helpful. Don't write your letters in such a way that the people receiving them feel that you considered it a chore to answer at all. Answer so that the persons receiving your letters "warm up" to them and are completely satisfied with the message.

The second thought is to be *courteous,* and I am sure I don't have to tell you to be that. You wouldn't be otherwise. Remember, however, that being courteous doesn't mean being formal or standoffish. It does mean using such expressions as "thank you," "we are sorry," "we are very glad"—*and meaning them.*

The third way is to be *human.* By that I mean—be *yourself.* But here again you must be the one to *put the brakes on.* By being yourself, I mean to write as you talk, "unbend" a little, be friendly. Don't unbend to the point where your letters become undignified, facetious, or fresh. Make people say when they read your letters, "It's certainly a pleasure to do business with that company. They always seem so interested."

With every letter you write, you have an opportunity to

make friends, to build good will. But to write *letters that make friends,* you must be sympathetic to the needs, thoughts, and wishes of the persons receiving them; you must be *courteous,* and you must be *human.*

One of the biggest obstacles to achieving personality and sincerity in a letter is the wrong balance in personal pronouns. Don't let your letters become lopsided in either direction. A letter with too many "we-our-us" phrases can't have personality and one with too many "you-yours" doesn't sound sincere.

When the "we-our-us" words and phrases stick out like so many sore thumbs it's because you're telling the story from your side of the fence. The reader is NOT interested in your problems or in you half so much as he's interested in how you're going to help him solve his problems, whatever they may be. But don't make the mistake of having your letters "you" heavy. What we want is a proper balance between the two—"you" and "we."

Notice how the "we's" stand out in this letter.

We are writing for permission to transfer the credit for the ironing board and curtain stretcher from your account to that of Mrs. Johnson, Summerville, New Jersey.

May *we* please have your cooperation regarding these credits.

We shall hold adjustments pending your reply.

How much friendlier it is when phrased this way—

May we please have permission to transfer the credit for the ironing board and curtain stretcher from your account to that of Mrs. Johnson, Summerville, New Jersey?

Your cooperation will be very much appreciated.

How to Make a Hit with Your Boss

It's simple. Just start writing *friendlier* letters.

Every *really friendly* letter you write will build good will in direct proportion to the sincerity and friendliness you put into it.

And that attitude, you can be sure, will *bear fruit*.

Watch for signs of it in your incoming letters. Notice the increasing evidence of appreciation on the part of your customers and prospects. Every once in a while, you'll see something like this—"It's certainly nice to do business with a company like yours. I feel you really have our interests at heart."

There's a lot of satisfaction in that for *you* and don't think your boss will be mad about it either.

Dear Sir:

The writer was pleased to notice your selection of our bank as the depository for your funds.

This is to inform you of our desire to make your relationship with us mutually pleasant and profitable. Our ambition is to offer you an informal, highly efficient service which will fully meet all of your banking requirements. We offer every service consistent with sound banking practice. As comparatively few people know of the many ways in which a modern bank may be of help to them, we are enclosing herewith a folder which describes the service which we are equipped to offer you.

Trusting you will find in this folder additional ways in which the Smith National may be of assistance to you, we remain

Very truly yours,

Here's a suggested revision. See if you don't agree it makes a more favorable impression.

Dear Mr. Johnson:

Our sincere thanks for the new account you opened with us yesterday.

I think you will find that we can fully meet all of your banking needs. And you can be sure that we shall do everything possible to make your relationship with us pleasant and profitable.

It has been my experience that few people realize the extent to which their bank can be of service. For that reason, we prepared a folder that describes the many ways that we might be of help to you. You'll find included every service consistent with sound banking practice.

This is your bank now and I hope you will make full use of its many facilities.

                                        Sincerely,

Assignment. *Make an analysis of one day's (or one week's) carbons of letters you've written recently and see if they have the qualities necessary to make friends. Check the "we-our-us" pronouns and see if they are in balance with the "you" pronouns. (They should be about 50-50.)*

Point No. 3. Watch Your Language

This third pointer can best be illustrated by a poem:

> *We beg to advise you* and *wish to state*
> That yours has arrived *of recent date.*
> We have it before us, *the contents noted,*
> *Herewith enclosed* are the prices quoted.
> Attached you will find, *as per your request,*
> The samples you want and *we would suggest*

Regarding the matter, and due to the fact
That up to this moment your order we've lacked
We hope that you will not delay it *unduly,*
And we *beg to remain, yours very truly.*

Bad paragraphing
First paragraph
should be
short

Stereo typed
opening

"Send" would
be better

Too much
WE

Dear Sir:

This will acknowledge receipt of your letter of
March 23, concerning the claim for your son, a
student at the above mentioned academy. We are
forwarding your letter to Mr. Knight's office and
suggest that if you have any medical bills in your
possession, and have not already done so, please
forward them to Mr. Knight's office for handling.
We have in our files a claim report from the
Suffield Academy submitted through Mr. Knight's
office and our only other explanation for the delay
in payment would be that the doctor has not ~~as yet~~
submitted a bill.

We regret any inconvenience caused you ~~on this~~
~~matter,~~ however, you may be assured that when
Mr. Knight's office is in possession of all the
facts in the case that your claim will receive
prompt and courteous attention.

Very truly yours,

insincere

lacks believability

all one sentence
and too long

There is a real opportunity for cleaning house in most of
our letter-writing vocabularies. Stereotyped, trite, hackneyed
phrases have no place in letter writing, primarily because
they serve no useful purpose. More important, they make it
difficult, if not impossible, for you to create the *favorable
impression* we are seeking. Let me give you some examples of
these *"relics of the past"* that you should try to get rid of, with
a suggested revision for each:

REPLYING TO YOUR LETTER
   Thank you for your letter

PLEASE BE ADVISED WE HAVE NO INFORMATION
   Sorry, but we have no information, etc.

WE ARE ATTACHING HERETO COPY, ETC.
   We are attaching copy

WE REGRET
   We are sorry

WE WISH TO APOLOGIZE
   We apologize

WE ARE FORWARDING UNDER SEPARATE COVER
   We are sending, separately, etc.

WE WISH TO ADVISE YOU (YOU ARE ADVISED)
   Instead of this, start right in telling them

THE WRITER WISHES TO ACKNOWLEDGE
   We acknowledge, etc.

Why do they do it? They don't talk that way. On the phone they sound like pretty good fellows. But once they get a stenographer in front of them, they give out with the same overworked, cold, lifeless, stereotyped words and phrases their great-great-grandfather used.

What's wrong with such words? They're cold, meaningless. They don't sound like YOU. They keep your letters from being friendly and sincere.

Let's get believability and sincerity in our letters. You say, *"We regret to advise you." Why,* when you know that people will know you don't mean it? Wouldn't it be better to say *"We are sorry,"* as if you *did* mean it?

"We regret any inconvenience which may have been caused" suggests a situation wherein you are at fault. If you

are going to say, therefore, that you are sorry for the delay or inconvenience, say it so he'll know you *are sorry.*

A Test That Never Fails

The very next time letters are brought to your desk for signing, read one of them out loud. Visualize yourself *saying* what you've written, to someone on the telephone. *How does it sound?* If you've used a lot of outdated words and stilted phrases, we warn you it'll sound ridiculous. But if you've written *naturally,* it will sound pretty much the same as a personally conveyed message would sound—friendly, sincere, natural. Read this letter aloud and you'll see what we mean:

> Dear Joe:
> I'll be very glad to have lunch with you on Tuesday and will plan to come over on the 10:00 train.
> That should bring me to your office just about noon.
> Cordially,

Try this test some time and see how *your* letters stack up. We think you'll find it helpful.

Assignment. *Take half a dozen carbons of letters you've written and circle the stereotyped words and phrases. Resolve not to use such words in future letters.*

Point No. 4. Don't Beat around the Bush

This pointer is about the *unnecessary* words in your letters. There are two good reasons why you should cut them down to a minimum.

One is the potential saving. Words cost money. They take time to dictate, typewrite, and read. *Let's make them count!* When you've taken forty words to say something that might have been better said in twenty, you have unconsciously taken money out of the firm's bank account and thrown it to the four winds. Remember—the cost of a dictated letter in the mail, including dictator's time, stenographic time, stationery, postage, etc., is usually around $1.50. That can run into a lot of money in annual correspondence cost, so it pays to use words sparingly.

Second, by eliminating unnecessary words, you make your letters *easier* to read, easier for the recipient to grasp the message. Whatever you have to say may be difficult to explain anyway. It becomes doubly hard for a person to understand what you are talking about if you take too many words to say it. When people don't understand, they have to write back, and that *doubles* the cost of the correspondence. Here are some examples of the *"long"* and the *"short"* of it.

This is to advise you that the new address has been noted on our records and future checks covering interest on these bonds will be directed in your care as Department Commander, Box 700, Somerville, Pennsylvania. (36 words)

As you requested, future checks covering interest on these bonds will be directed to your attention as Department Commander, Box 700, Somerville, Pennsylvania. (23 words)

* * *

We appreciate very much your interest and active participation in our program, and if we can assist further in this matter, please feel free to write again. (27 words)

Your interest and participation in our program are appreciated. If we can help further, please feel free to write again. (20 words)

* * *

We deeply regret the inconvenience which has been caused you in the process of adjusting our records. (17 words)

We are sorry there has been so much difficulty adjusting our records. (12 words)

*   *   *

At the present time (4 words)
At present (2 words)

*   *   *

Thank you for your check for $62, which has been placed to your credit. (14 words)
Thank you for your check for $62. (7 words)

*   *   *

We do not feel that we can afford (8 words)
We cannot afford (3 words)

In CHANGING TIMES, the Kiplinger Magazine, there was one of the best short articles on letter writing I've seen in a long while. With the editor's permission I am reproducing part of it here.

Every time you write a letter, you paint a portrait of yourself. Look at these two samples. See how a few words, identical in meaning, can draw two completely different pictures.

First, consider this: "I am at present engaged in the sale of corn on commission. It is not an avocation of a remunerative description."

Got the picture of the man who said that? O.K. Now suppose precisely the same thought had been expressed in these words: "I sell corn on commission. It does not pay."

You get a picture of quite a different person, don't you? The first man is windy and pompous. The second is forceful and direct.

They *were* different people, too. The first was Micawber, the famed blowhard in Dickens' *David Copperfield*. The second was a businessman who revised Micawber's words into uncluttered English.

Let's see how that transformation of Micawber's statement took place. It was a simple but instructive process. Two basic rules of letter writing were applied.

1. Don't use needless words
2. Get to the point

Here's how needless words were pruned from Micawber's prose. *"Engaged in the sale of"* means *"sell."* That one word does the work of Micawber's five. *"I am at present"* means he's doing it *right now*. Well, you could say *"now"* instead of *"at present"* and make a 50% saving on the deal. But *"I am now selling corn"* is still too wordy. Why say *"now"* when *"I am selling"* means selling now? And why use that when the simplest form of all, *"I sell,"* carries the full meaning of present action?

Now take the next sentence. What's wrong with saying, *"It is not an avocation of a remunerative description?"* That sentence is weak because it describes the point instead of stating it. If selling corn doesn't pay, why not say so? Can you imagine the FBI saying, "Crime is not an occupation likely to yield large returns?"

Old Micawber had one saving grace. After rambling a while, he finally would get to the point by saying *"in short . . ."* or *"in other words . . ."* In the sample we used he did go on to say, "In other words, it does not pay."

You can use the same trick to analyze and improve *your* letters.

Assignment. *Take another six carbons and examine them carefully for unnecessary "beating around the bush." Edit them with this one pointer in mind.*

Point No. 5. Get Off to a Good Start

This pointer has to do with *how to start a letter.* Next to the physical form of the letter, the one big thing which influences that important *"first impression"* is the opening sentence.

It is probably one of the most vital points in a letter, for on it depends to an extent the *"frame of mind"* in which your reader tackles the rest of the letter. If the reaction to your message depends on the right frame of mind, as in the case of an answer to an inquiry or a settlement of a complaint, then it is doubly important that the way be prepared by a friendly, courteous approach.

If you're going to write better letters, the place to start is at the beginning—with the first thing you say after that meaningless but time-honored salutation: "Dear Mr. Smith." Here is where you begin to show what kind of person you are, what kind of company you represent. From the very first sentence, the recipient of your letter begins to form an *impression,* just as you do when you first meet someone. You want that first impression to be favorable and that's why the opening sentence is so important.

We wrote to a New York client the other day for an appointment. His reply started out: "Yes, of course I'll be glad to see you next Friday afternoon." Sounds *friendly,* doesn't it? Suppose he had written, "The writer wishes to acknowledge your letter of the 10th and in reply would state that

Friday afternoon will be satisfactory." Do you see the difference in the mental *picture* you receive from the two replies?

Make your first paragraph *do something* besides just letting the recipient know you're answering his letter. He knows that anyway. Keep these four ways in mind when dictating first sentences and you'll have no trouble in getting your letters off to a flying start:

1. *Express pleasure or regret.* Examples:
   "Thank you for your letter. It was appreciated."

   or

   "Sorry, but we are afraid it is impossible to grant your request."

2. *Show that some action has been taken.* Examples:
   "Your request of December 10th has already been taken care of."

   or

   "Just as soon as your letter of the 10th came in we took immediate steps to, etc."

3. *Ask or answer a question.* Examples:
   "May we have some additional information?"

   or

   "Yes, we shall be glad to make the changes you requested in your letter of—."

4. *Give some news.* Example:
   "You will be interested to learn that (etc.) . . ."

Here are some examples of opening sentences to *avoid:*

We have received your letter of December 10th.
(He knows you have or you wouldn't be answering it.)

* * *

Replying to your letter of the 22nd, would state that . . .

(Lacks friendliness, warmth and courtesy. Does nothing but acknowledge the letter.)

* * *

Acknowledging (or responding to) your letter of the 10th inst.

(Same criticism applies.)

* * *

I have before me your letter of the 21st.

(Doesn't mean anything. What does he care?)

* * *

Your communication of the 21st has been referred to me.

(Why tell him the obvious?)

* * *

We have carefully noted your letter of the 23rd.

(Lacks sincerity. Sounds cold and severe.)

* * *

Regarding your letter of the 10th.

(Does nothing but acknowledge, when it should be putting the reader in the right frame of mind.)

Beware of Complex Openings

Whether you're writing a sales letter or the routine every-day kind of letter, start off with an easy-to-read opening paragraph containing *one* idea. Don't blurt out five or six ideas all at once, like this letter from a large department store.

Dear Customer:

It has never been so important to take care of your furs as it is now, when fur prices are rising daily. Because of this, we are writing our own customers now, so they may be assured of space in the famous (name of store) Fur Storage Vaults this summer. Even though these vaults are the largest in Pennsylvania, they have filled so quickly in past years that many customers could not be accommodated, and we suggest you make your arrangements now.

How much better, *stronger,* it is when broken up, like this—

Dear Customer:

With fur prices rising daily, it has never been more important to take care of your furs than now.

That is why we are writing you this month—so that *you may be sure of space in the famous (name of store) Fur Storage Vaults this summer.*

Even though these vaults are the largest in Pennsylvania, they have filled so quickly in past years that many customers could not be accommodated, so we suggest you make your arrangements now.

Write as you talk. A letter is *you* in print. It used to be that "the only letters to display symptoms of red-blooded authorship were either love letters or the controversial letters of statesmen." It's different now. Modern times demand modern methods—and modern letters. One way to make sure they'll be modern is to *"get off on the right foot"* by means of a useful, friendly, courteous first sentence.

The First Sentence Sets the Pace

What you say in your first sentence, and the friendliness and sincerity with which you say it, usually establish the keynote for the whole letter. Here are some examples of good openings—see if you don't agree they get the letter off to a fine start.

Thank you for your thoughtfulness in writing as you did on October 10th, and for sending in the unit that disappointed you.

Thank you very much for your inquiry. We appreciate your interest.

You are entirely correct. We did ship you the wrong color and are very sorry indeed.

I find that I'm coming up your way next Tuesday. Could you possibly arrange to see me some time in the morning?

Assignment. *Memorize the four types of openings and write two of each for your own kind of letters.*

How about a "Dearless" Letter?

For some time now there has been considerable discussion and controversy over the subject of *"Dearless"* letters. More and more people feel we should drop the ancient, stereotyped and meaningless word *"Dear"* in the salutation. Many conservative companies are bound by tradition and are, in the vernacular, stuck with it. To change all their letters from "Dear Mr. Smith" to some such opening as "Thank you very much, Mr. Smith" might tend to make them conspicuous.

But just to keep you abreast of things, the movement is growing. And it will probably continue to gain momentum. The desire to get away from meaningless words and phrases in correspondence is strong, even with those who prefer not to take the lead. If you're the courageous type, however, here are some examples of *dearless* openings and a list of things to avoid:

Thank you very much, Mr. Smith,
for the helpful information given in your letter.

You are absolutely right, Mr. Jones,
in complaining about etc.

Since receiving your letter, Mr. Brown,
we've tried to get the information you need.

That problem of yours, Mr. Drake,
will require some study but etc.

It is a pleasure, Mrs. Taylor,
to explain the item that isn't too clear etc.

1. Don't try to force this style down the throat of management. Wait until those concerned are convinced. Don't force it on everyone you write to. If writing to a bank president for example, or people you suspect are stuffed shirts, take it easy.

2. Naturally you'll avoid any tendency towards flippancy such as "Hi there, Mr. Whosis." Sounds like an unnecessary caution but it's been done.

3. Keep the opening phrase as short as you can—three or four words if possible. Of course, not counting the man's name.

4. Shy from negative approaches like "We're disappointed, Mr. Customer."

5. It's best not to use numerals in the opener and shun the use of quotations—slang—too much punctuation.

Point No. 6. Make a Graceful Exit

The next pointer is on when to *stop dictating*. The answer can be summed up very quickly. *Stop when you have finished saying what you have to say*. Avoid participial endings, such as "Hoping you will appreciate our position in the matter, we are"; "Thanking you, we remain," etc.

The participial ending is old-fashioned. It lacks definiteness, serves no particular purpose, has been *"done to death"* by the pounding of a billion typewriter keys.

One of the surest tests of a good letter is to read it aloud—see if it sounds natural—see if it might be somewhat like your own conversation, were your customer or prospect right across the desk from you. If the person addressed *were* there, how would it sound if you finished your talk with "Hoping this meets with your approval, I beg to remain . . ."? If you only knew how much more power, friendliness, and warmth you can put into your letters just by closing them simply and naturally, you'd never use a stereotyped ending again, participial or otherwise.

Stop with a direct statement. Then the last thing read by the recipient of your letter will *mean something*. It should be an integral part of the letter and worthy of the space it occupies rather than a meaningless jargon that steals time from the dictator and stenographer, only to waste it again on the reader.

Let's take some examples:

"Hoping you will appreciate our position in the matter, we are"

might be better expressed

"Does this satisfactorily explain our position? If not please let us know."

* * *

"Thanking you, we remain"

might be better expressed

"Thank you very much,"

or just

"Thank you"

* * *

"Awaiting your reply with interest, we remain"

might be better expressed

"We shall be very glad to hear from you."

These suggestions are purely illustrative. Many other expressions might be equally effective. The thing to remember is that, according to psychological tests, the first and last impressions are frequently more important than those received in between. With this in mind, let's make the letter *"good to the last word."*

What about the Closing?

Please drop the meaningless closers like "Yours very truly," "Very truly yours" and "Yours truly," and begin right now to use words that serve a useful purpose. Like *"Sincerely."* Or *"Cordially,"* if you have some acquaintance with the person to whom you're writing. Some of our more modern letter writers are eliminating the usual closer altogether and in its place saying *"Best regards"* or *"Good luck to you."* I don't recommend going that far in everyday business letters but I do hope you'll change at least to *"Sincerely"* if you're not already using it. It describes exactly the way in which the letter it closes *should* have been written.

Assignment. *Examine at least six of your own letters to see how they stack up in the close.*

Point No. 7. Plan Your Work—Organize Your Facts

Want to know how to become a better dictator? You can really sum up the answer in two words—*better planning.* And that simply means doing a better job of *getting ready to dictate.*

What happens with many of us is that we suddenly become conscious of a pile of letters on our desk looking at us reproachfully as if to say "Hurry, hurry, we need to be answered." When we can't put it off any longer, we buzz for a secretary or stenographer, or turn to a dictating machine and start grinding them out—thinking all the while of the *hundreds* of other equally (?) or more (?) important details that we are neglecting. That's a bad habit, of course, and not conducive to good letter writing. So, to help you get ready to dictate, here is a

Six-point System

● Read *carefully* each letter to be answered, making notes in the margin or on a separate pad, of the parts that must be answered. Underscore or number important items.

● Collect all the material you will need. Send to the files for previous correspondence. Get prices or other pertinent information.

● If *you* have a decision to make, think over all the facts, analyze the problem, decide what you are going to do, then note it. If someone else must make the decision, find out what it is and make a note on the letter or in an attached memo.

● Ask yourself exactly what you want the letter to accomplish. What do you want the reader to do when he has finished reading your letter? Do you merely want him to say to himself, "Okay, that takes care of *that*," and be perfectly satisfied and happy about it? Or do you want him to take some kind of action, and if so—*what?*

● Rough out in your own mind, if not on paper, what you are going to say. Decide what points should be covered and plan to present them in logical order. Try to visualize the person to whom you are writing. Does the picture you get in your mind suggest an informal kind of approach, pleasantly busi-ness-like, or dignified, but not stuffy?

● Finally, make a mental check. Is your proposed letter *com-plete?* Does it answer *all* the questions, cover *all* the points, anticipate the needs of the recipient so far as practical? Will it make a *favorable* impression?

Now, you're ready to write a letter, and chances are it will be a very good one. The planning procedure sounds involved but so do the functions of almost every operation when you list them separately. Familiarize yourself, however, with what is just a routine process for the expert letter writer and you'll soon be doing all these things *automatically*.

Point No. 8. Be Sure You Say What You Mean

This pointer has to do not so much with *what* you say, but *how* you say it. It's about the TONE in your letters. Wars have been waged, fights have been fought, and business lost in abundance because of an unintentional use of the wrong tone. Frequently we write letters with the best of intentions and with nothing—but the friendliest of thoughts—yet our atti-tude is misinterpreted and somebody gets *"miffed."* Wrong tone.

When a man talking to us face to face wins our complete confidence, we often say, "His frankness won us over." What we usually mean is, his friendliness, his sincerity, his whole attitude won us over, for these are the things that inspire confidence.

All are *personal* qualities. A stone wall can't be friendly or sincere. Nor can a typewritten sheet of paper. You can't make a letter ring with sincerity unless you make it sound like a real person. *It must have personality.*

If you agree with that, you'll also agree that personality re-quires *two* people—one to radiate it and one to reflect it.

A letter that talks entirely about you and your interests can have but very little personality, for there is no real reader interest to reflect it. Most folks are essentially selfish—they are interested in you or your proposition only insofar as it affects *them*. They want to be talked to in their own language, not yours. *The same psychological laws* that create liking and trust between two persons in conversation create liking and trust in a letter.

Write your message as far as possible with the other fellow's viewpoint in mind. Be what they call *"an understanding cuss,"* for you never met one yet who didn't make friends easily.

Don't let your letters be all *"we-our-us"* or all *"you and your."* Both angles are too one-sided to be effective. It's the "you and I" or "yours and ours" attitude that we want, for that's probably what it would be if your reader were right across the desk from you.

Look for the personality in this letter:

> We take pleasure in acknowledging your acceptance of the agency for the sale of our goods, and we hereby confirm the arrangements made with you by our traveling agent.
>
> We hardly need to say that our products, which have been in general use for over fifteen years, will always prove to be what they are represented.
>
> Whenever it is practicable, it will be well for you to have them tried side by side with other brands, so that your customers can judge for themselves of the superiority of our goods.

That is a message, but there certainly isn't much *personality* in it. Let's rewrite it and see if we can't make it do a better public relations job:

We are very glad to confirm the arrangements made with you by our Mr. Brown for the sale of Jones products. You will, we feel sure, find the agency a pleasant and profitable one.

Jones products have been in general use for over fifteen years. They enjoy a fine reputation for both quality and dependability. What is particularly important to you, they *repeat*. Customers invariably like them and come back for more.

Sales literature to help you sell is enclosed. If there is anything else you need, please don't hesitate to ask for it.

There isn't anything gushy about that, yet you'll agree it sounds sincere, as though you were glad to be helpful.

Every letter that leaves your desk gives a *"picture"* of your company. Every letter you send out helps someone decide what kind of an organization it is, takes him closer or pushes him further away from a decision to buy. Every contact you have with the public can have its influence on company good will. Every word, sentence, and paragraph in your letters have their effect. Because you can't *see* the effect of your words, it is doubly important that the tone be calculated to aid rather than hinder the message. By writing as you talk, by being natural and friendly and sincere and *"human"* in your dictating, you can have *every* letter make a loyal friend for the firm and a booster for its products.

Assignment. *Rewrite one of your typical letters and try to improve its tone.*

Point No. 9. Stay away from Non-stop Sentence Derbys

Stay away from long sentences—*they're dangerous!* They're like barbed-wire entanglements—you get in, and before you get out, you've cut the clarity of your message to ribbons. And made it difficult for the letter to make friends.

I've seen any quantity of letters that were excellent except in one respect—the extreme length of some of the sentences.

This simply makes the letter harder to read and understand and therefore less effective.

It's bad enough when long sentences are written by one of the relatively few people who have the happy faculty of being able to express themselves clearly no matter how long it takes. On the other hand, when an inexperienced letter writer attempts the lengthy sentence, the usual result is a confused, unintelligible conglomeration of words—not a clearcut message at all.

Look at this 123-word sentence:

> Upon receipt of your letter of July 20, 1956, with a copy of a letter dated July 10, 1956, addressed to you by the Eastern Bank and Trust Company, requesting that bonds which had been issued in the form "John Jones, Trustee Under the Will of Marion P. Smith, Deceased, for the benefit of A. S. Brown," be reissued to substitute the words "in trust for" for the words "for the benefit of" in the inscription, we wrote to the Eastern Bank and Trust Company asking them to submit a reference to any previous correspondence with the Treasury Department since they appeared to be under the impression that Mr. Jones received permission to use the form of registration which they requested.

Here's one that contains 109 words without a single stop.

> Replying to your letter received several days ago in reference to a purchase of curtains which you advise were not as ordered, we are indeed sorry for the annoyance you

have had in this occasion and we have issued a call to have the merchandise returned to us and upon receipt of same we will have credited to your account and we would appreciate it very much if you will kindly advise the description of the curtains you originally ordered as to price, size and color and we will be very glad to try to fill your order and again regretting extremely the error we have made, we are,

Here's another—a 53-word sentence, not as long as the others, but still *too long:*

It is generally known that New England agriculture is in an extremely sound condition, and with the twenty-two million dollars now available for the use of New England farmers through the Agricultural Relief Bill, advertisers will find it to their benefit to carefully consider the New England farm market for their products.

Now read the words that Abraham Lincoln wrote in his 1861 farewell address at Springfield and see how close the periods are.

My Friends: No one not in my situation can appreciate my feeling of sadness at this parting. To this place and the kindness of these people I owe everything. Here I have lived a quarter of a century and have passed from a young to an old man. Here my children have been born and one is buried. I now leave, not knowing when or whether ever I may return, with a task before me greater than that which rested upon Washington. . . .

How wonderfully clear-cut and concise! How easy to understand! After all, there's no secret about it. Cultivate the habit of breaking up the message into smaller doses—that's all. The following example shows how easy it is to break up long sentences.

Original sentence:

In reply to your note of recent date with copy to Dr. Johnson of Mont., Ala. this letter is just what I wanted, inasmuch as I have been over all the points with him, and when he receives your letter it acts as a check on what I told him and therefore as a return call.

Analysis of a Sales Letter

First paragraph too long - uninviting - complicated

STEREOTYPED
See words underscored

(We) are enclosing <u>herewith</u> our new No. 8 Rate Card, which goes into effect with the July issue of MODERN GARDENING. (Our) circulation has increased from 70,000 to over 100,000 or an increase of 40%. Naturally, this new card represents an adjustment of the rates to give effect to this increase in circulation. In the meantime, advertising in the May and June issues remains at the old rates based on a circulation of 70,000 but yet the actual circulation in those two months will be about 90,000 for May and 95,000 for June, thus giving an extra dividend for advertising in those two months.

all one sentence - 51 words. Too long to be grasped quickly

Beginning with the July issue, (we) are not going to be content to remain at 100,000 and there will be a steady increase in circulation, which will not be adjusted in the advertising rates until the coming January issue. Thus, practically every issue next year will carry an extra dividend of circulation.

Too much we-our- as See words circled

(We) wish to advise also, that this increase of circulation is not being obtained through high pressure, door to door subscription crew workers. [It is 100% being obtained] through the mailing to high class horticulture lists. (We) know from letters that (we) receive from satisfied advertisers that (we) have a very fine readership which responds wonderfully to advertising in MODERN GARDENING.

Poor Construction

Remember, this is not an increase in the cost of your advertising, for you are merely paying for increased circulation which has cost us a tremendous sum of money to obtain, and for the cost of the increased number of magazines we now have to print.

ADDITIONAL COMMENTS

Too many statistics in first two paragraphs Letter doesn't sufficiently sell the magazine

Rewritten:

The copy of letter to Dr. Johnson, enclosed with your note dated April 2nd, is just what I wanted. I have been all over the points with him and when he receives your letter it will check perfectly with what I told him.

Try it out on your next letter. Be sure, however, to keep in mind that sentences must follow in logical sequence and read smoothly.

Assignment. *Rewrite the following paragraph using shorter sentences. Then notice how much easier it is both to read and to understand.*

Most buyers, like you and me, like to feel that we are obtaining a high-grade product and full value for the money paid and both of us know that advertised products are generally specified and always demanded in preference to ones not so well known because of lack of complete advertising, even though the quality of the product contained in a cheaper and flimsier paper box may be equally as good or better than the advertised product.

Point No. 10. Realize the Opportunity in Inquiry Letters

We are concerned now with two kinds of letters. One is the kind that *asks* for information; the other the kind that *gives* it. The one *asking* for information we will call the *"inquiry"* letter. Let's talk first about that—the one you send out to get information.

Put down these three things: (1) *what* is wanted, (2) *who* wants it, and (3) *why* it is wanted. *What, who,* and *why!* Keep in mind the necessity for removing all confusion in the recipient's mind as to what you desire. *And be concise.* Again let me urge you to think in terms of the recipient and give him or her the information that you yourself would want if you were on the receiving end. That shouldn't be difficult, because you are familiar with all the facts. The people to whom you write know little or nothing about your business or its problems. Make things clear to them. Ask questions that can be answered by a yes or no, if possible. Make it easy for the simplest minded person to understand your request and give you the information needed.

One manufacturer who was having trouble with his incoming inquiries inserted the following article in his monthly house organ:

A WASTE OF TIME AND EFFORT

In these strenuous times, it is necessary to eliminate lost time and motion wherever possible, so that every ounce of effort will *count.*

With this in mind, we are prompted to mention the importance of making every inquiry *complete,* to eliminate the necessity for writing back for additional information.

Below are two examples showing the style of inquiry referred to:

"One of our customers uses large quantities of White Gummed Paper and we would like to have samples and prices of your product."

"Please quote us on Red Gummed Paper in sheets."

In each instance it was necessary for us to write back for additional information because we had no lead as to what was required in regard to the following:

Quantity
Size

Length or diameter (if on rolls)
Color
Finish
Basic weight
Gumming

We have in our line 51 kinds of White Gummed Paper and 27 different colors and in most instances each of them is furnished with two kinds of gumming and many are furnished in two sizes. Thus it will be seen that unless inquiries completely cover the points mentioned above, it becomes necessary for us to write back for more information, thus causing delay and routine congestion.

Let's talk now about your *answers* to inquiries, to those people writing in for information. In the writing of these letters it is even more important to write *from the recipient's side of the fence*. It is easier for people to grasp information that is given to them in terms of what it means to *them*. Size up the needs of the inquirer, and answer accordingly. Be complete; give *all* the information requested. And give *more*, if you feel it would be helpful.

If you can anticipate a question or provide any additional facts that you feel would be useful to the inquirer without going to extremes, by all means do it. Remember, we are thinking not only in terms of giving information, *but also of doing a public relations job*. If there is anything to go with the letter, send it along at the same time if possible, instead of under separate cover. Make sure that the inquirer's name and address are spelled correctly.

Here's a Cold One for You

Following is a letter exactly as it was received, written by a man who, you'll agree, doesn't know (a) how to write a friendly letter or (b) how to answer an inquiry. Here's the letter—

> We are pleased to enclose herewith our booklet #88 which we trust you will find of interest.
>
> Hoping to be favored with your valued orders and always with pleasure at your service, we remain,

If you deliberately tried, it would be difficult to get so many meaningless phrases in such a short letter. Who could possibly get *anything* good out of expressions like *"we are pleased"*—*"hoping to be favored with your valued orders"*— *"we remain,"* etc. More important, the letter falls far short as an adequate answer to an inquiry. All it says, really, is "You asked for a booklet. Here it is. Goodbye."

Not a word of thanks for the inquiry, no mention of the product and what it might do for the prospect, no highlighting of sales features, no offer of additional information, no suggestion that might lead to *action*.

Here is a good answer to an inquiry. Notice how completely it anticipates and answers questions that are undoubtedly in the inquirer's mind.

> Thank you for your recent inquiry about mail order advertising in HOLIDAY. I am delighted to know you are considering our fine publication for one of your clients, and it is a pleasure to send the information you requested.
>
> To show you how appropriate HOLIDAY is for recreation and sporting equipment advertising, I have assembled some pertinent material for you in the enclosed folder.
>
> First, the "Highlights on HOLIDAY Families"—an introduction to the unusual people who comprise our audience. The leisure activities of our readers—fishing, sailing, boating, etc.—their vacation habits, and their high

income all combine to make them excellent prospects for products and services that contribute to relaxation and to pleasure.

Following this are two results stories, the first one on the Klepper Co. We were told that this advertiser was especially pleased with the *quality* of HOLIDAY inquiries and with the low conversion cost. I understand that this firm has recently expanded its retail operation, and at the same time, has temporarily reduced its national advertising expenditure. Then, although Acushnet's Golf Balls are rather removed from boating equipment, the fact that their HOLIDAY advertising produced such outstanding results indicates that other high-priced merchandise in the sports equipment field could also be sold profitably through HOLIDAY.

No doubt you are familiar with many of the firm names listed under the "Boats and Marine Equipment" heading of the Holiday Advertisers by Classification list I've included. However, you might be interested to know that HOLIDAY is the only general publication used year after year by several of these leading companies.

HOLIDAY, with its long history of advertising gains (each year has shown an increase in linage and revenue over the previous year, with last year the biggest yet), is a natural medium for anything that will make our readers' lives, hobbies, holidays more enjoyable, more exciting. And THE HOLIDAY SHOPPER, our mail order advertising section, is the natural choice for those advertisers whose unusual or quality products and services are sold by mail. Our special, low rate for mail order advertising, plus copy and cut requirements, closing dates and other details are explained on the attached rate sheet.

I am sending you also, under separate cover, a copy of

our November issue which is now on the newsstands and our June issue. The Chris-Craft advertisement on the back cover of June is one which might be of special interest to you.

It will be a pleasure to work with you on your boating client's advertising, and if you have any questions or would like additional information, please do let me know.

Sincerely,

Assignment. *Go into your file again, find a request for information and an answer to an inquiry—see how they stack up with the foregoing points in mind.*

Point No. 11. Write a Satisfying Answer

If there's one thing a person hates to get in the mail, it's an unsatisfactory or *incomplete* answer to his letter.

Many letters contain two, three, or even more separate and distinct questions. If at all possible, *answer all of them*. If you can't answer some, at least say why you can't, but don't just ignore them.

After you've written your letter, read it just as carefully as you read the one it answers. Then ask yourself—have you written a really complete and satisfying answer? Have you replied to *all* his questions and given him *all* the information he requested? Is your letter friendly, courteous, sincere, and to the point? Is there anything in it that will help to build good will?

Is there anything in it by which he could possibly be antagonized? Can you shorten it in any way, without making it less complete or less friendly? Is it attractively set up and inviting in physical appearance?

The answer to a letter requesting information is one of the

most important letters in your routine correspondence. It's the open door, many times, to thousands of dollars' worth of new business.

Remember, in *all* your letters you mold opinions *for* or *against*. You make friends or you create enemies; you make people sore or you turn them into enthusiastic boosters. *It's up to you.*

Point No. 12. Be Careful How You Answer Complaints

Probably the most difficult letter you will ever be asked to write is the answer to a complaint. Each one your company receives represents a serious potential loss, for if you don't handle it properly, you stand to lose not only the complainant's business, but more besides. *A disgruntled customer loves to talk.*

Complaints are caused by a number of things—

1. Something you *say* that doesn't sit right.
2. Something you *do* which seems to the customer unreasonable, unnecessary, or inexcusable.
3. Something, a condition or act, over which you have no control whatever.
4. Perhaps just a misunderstanding.

Let's talk for a minute about the first—something you *say* which doesn't sit right. Perhaps the word *"inadvertently"* should be in there, for surely you don't say something *on purpose* that might offend or make a customer sore.

But, maybe you used a *"red"* word, so called because it usually makes the reader *see* red. Such words as:

claim, as in the sentence "We have your letter in which you claim that the whoosis we sent you arrived in damaged condition." Would that *sit well* with you? Sounds as though the writer doesn't believe you.

frankly, as in the sentence "Frankly, we can't understand your attitude." Sounds as though the writer got up on the wrong side of the bed.

contrary, as in the sentence "Contrary to your opinion, we are not in position to ship every order as soon as received." Sounds as though the writer doesn't care much whether he keeps his customers or not.

if, as in the sentence "If we are at fault, as your letter says, etc."

There are a lot more *red* words and phrases that you will do well to avoid if you want to keep complaints at a minimum. Here are just a few—"you state, you overlooked, you forgot, we cannot understand, failure, false, unfair, untrue, ignorant, etc."

We'll skip reasons 2 and 3 because they have nothing whatever to do with letters. But we can't skip number 4.

Misunderstandings don't just *happen.* They are caused by faulty expression on the part of the letter writer, or incomplete thinking through of the problem. Don't, please, forget that your job, in writing a letter, is not only to convey a message *but also to get it understood,* and the job isn't finished until the message *is* understood.

So much for the reasons *why* we receive complaints.

Now let's tackle the business of handling them. First, bear in mind that everything we've said in this book about writing as you would like to be written to, about stereotyped words and expressions, too much "we-our-us," etc., applies to *all* letters, *but particularly to the ones you write in answer to a complaint.*

First thing you do when a complaint letter comes in, of course, is to make an investigation.

Is it definitely *your* fault? Definitely *his* fault? Or one of those delicate borderline cases where it would be difficult to say accurately that *anyone* was at fault? It could easily have been caused by something beyond your control.

If it is your fault, the complaint can be satisfactorily handled by a very simple letter in which you come right out and say so—frankly admitting the mistake and making whatever adjustment is called for. Even in this comparatively simple type of letter, however, there is an opportunity to do a good public relations job for your company, or a bad one. If you're going to make an adjustment, make it *wholeheartedly*, not begrudgingly. If you're at fault in some way, you should be sorry. *Then say you're sorry in such a way that he'll know you mean it.* Don't use the completely insincere and meaningless sort of expression like "We deeply regret the inconvenience caused you by this unfortunate oversight." *Write it the way you'd say it!*

A harder problem exists where the complaint is justified but where nothing specific in the way of an adjustment is suggested. The customer is sore—and takes the attitude, *"What are you going to do about it?"* You must first determine how far to go in your adjustment and then decide how to tell him about it in such a way as to pacify him completely.

The hardest problem of all arises when you don't consider it wise to grant the demands of the complainant and must turn his view around to your way of thinking; you must refuse his request for an adjustment and *"make him like it."* The fact is that, when you are answering a complaint, it doesn't make any difference whether the person is right or not, justified or not, he *thinks* he is and that amounts to the same thing. Probably the easiest way I can illustrate how to handle a complaint is by drawing two straight lines. One line represents the complaint, coming in your direction. The other represents your answer to it. If your reply starts out with a "chip on its shoulder," *additional sparks will be the result.*

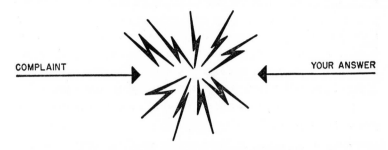

That will also be true if your letter is cold, indifferent, if it doesn't go *out of its way* to make friends. What it must do first of all is to *side-step the complainant's anger* or annoyance and get the discussion on a *friendly* basis.

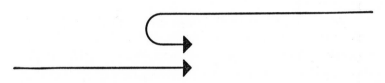

In other words, you must do an about-face and get *in step* with the complainant before there will be any chance of a satisfactory settlement. This you do by showing, through your attitude, that you appreciate his position—can easily understand why he would feel as he does—and that you are going to do everything possible to straighten things out.

Don't hesitate to say "Thank you" to a person sending in a complaint, particularly if it uncovers some shortcomings of yours. We should be glad for the opportunity to put our house in order. Also it is important that whatever you say or do to make amends for the condition which caused the complaint be said or done *wholeheartedly,* not *begrudgingly.*

Answer complaints as quickly as possible—don't keep people waiting any longer than necessary for at least a friendly acknowledgment. Of all the letters you write, the most important are the answers to complaints, and I personally would give them the "green light" over all others. One good reason is this: *The longer a man is angry about something the more chance he has to spread his anger around to other people.*

Read the following answer to a complaint that I made not long ago about my car. See if you don't agree it does a swell job of pacifying.

Thank you very much for your letter regarding your new Lincoln.

I appreciate very much your attitude in regard to the good and so-called "bad" points regarding your new car. Also, I appreciate your mentioning about Norman being most cooperative.

You asked for my opinion in regard to the noise and hard ride. I think the condition can from experience be traced to the Shock Absorbers rather than the tires. When you can spare the car, we will be very happy to install a complete new set of Shock Absorbers and feel sure that this will eliminate the hard ride.

Regarding tires, the General Sqeegie tire is a very good tire but I do not think the car is designed for a tire that heavy. While the manufacturer gives the correct amount of air pressure as 24 pounds, I think they have allowed for a slight build-up when driving on the open road.

The Radio Push Buttons being loose and vibrating continuously is not normal and I am sure can be corrected even if it means replacing with all new ones.

Please feel free to let us know, when the new Shock Absorbers have been installed, if this corrects the ride.

We are very anxious to have you most satisfied with this new Lincoln and are at your service at any time to make your driving a pleasure.

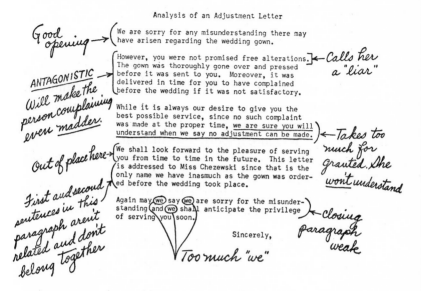

Analysis of an Adjustment Letter

Good opening → We are sorry for any misunderstanding there may have arisen regarding the wedding gown.

However, you were not promised free alterations. The gown was thoroughly gone over and pressed before it was sent to you. Moreover, it was delivered in time for you to have complained before the wedding if it was not satisfactory. ←*Calls her a "liar"*

ANTAGONISTIC → *Will make the person complaining even madder.*

While it is always our desire to give you the best possible service, since no such complaint was made at the proper time, we are sure you will understand when we say no adjustment can be made. ←*Takes too much for granted. She won't understand*

Out of place here→ We shall look forward to the pleasure of serving you from time to time in the future. This letter is addressed to Miss Chezewski since that is the only name we have inasmuch as the gown was ordered before the wedding took place.

First and second sentences in this paragraph aren't related and don't belong together

Again may (we) say (we) are sorry for the misunderstanding (and (we) shall anticipate the privilege of serving (you) soon.) ←*closing paragraph weak*

Sincerely,

↙ *Too much "we"*

Assignment. *Analyze two or three of your adjustment letters, and see if you have used the right psychology.*

Point No. 13. Make Collection Letters Sales Letters, Too

Letter writing in the accounting department is the same as in any other department, in at least one respect. *Every assignment has a dual objective*—to convey a message and to plant the seeds of friendship. Or, in the case of customers, to further the friendly feeling that already exists.

What incentive is there for salesmen to knock themselves out getting new customers, if they're going to be mistreated in the accounting department?

In the financial part of a business, the principal letter writing functions are these:

1. Establishing credit standing
2. Arranging for terms of payment
3. Collecting overdue accounts
4. Straightening out improper cash discounts
5. Giving credit information when requested

The last of these is, of course, a very simple assignment. The other four, however, call for extreme tact, understanding, and finesse. Such letters are as important as any sent out by the company, and more important than most.

How do you ask a man for bank and personal references in such a way that he doesn't take offense?

How do you tell a customer that his financial position doesn't justify credit and that he will therefore have to pay in advance?

How do you tell a customer that he will have to reimburse you for the $6.48 deducted four days after the cash discount date?

It's easy enough to write such letters if you don't care what happens to the customer. The trick is in being able to make the recipient see the fairness in your rules and be willing to abide by them. Each of the above calls for:

a. The realization that you have a *selling* job to do
b. The desire to keep the customer from getting mad and taking his business elsewhere
c. The ability to put yourself in the customer's place and anticipate his normal reaction to your message

Now let's talk about what is probably the most important job of all in the accounting department—*collecting money from overdue accounts.*

"John Doe is three months overdue, Bill. Write him a letter and jack him up." Bill dictates the letter in the usual way.

That's the procedure with some firms; with most it is a cut-and-dried proposition of pulling the card out of the file at a certain date, sending Form Letter No. 1, following it up so many days later, and systematically carrying it through to the point of either getting the money or bringing legal pressure to bear.

In either case, the letters sent are collection letters and are governed by the same common-sense rules. Whether you are familiar with them or not, it's a mighty good idea to review them now and then—simply to keep up to the highest possible efficiency—*for collection letters are important.* A sale isn't really a sale until the merchandise is paid for, because until then you are not only minus a profit but you are "out" the goods as well.

Start first with the fact that there are two objectives: to get the money and to keep the customer. Even if you decide that the customer isn't worth keeping, you must be extremely careful not to antagonize him. A disgruntled customer usually results in the loss of more business than his own.

Next classify your delinquent accounts into three groups: good customers and good pay, good customers but slow pay, questionable customers and poor pay.

Obviously, you wouldn't write the same kind of a letter to the third group as you would to the first, or write to the first as you would to the second. If you aren't sure whether a customer belongs in the second or third, give him the benefit of the doubt and treat him as a "good customer—slow pay" until you are *sure*.

There should be a series of collection letters—different in their appeal—to each of these three groups. There will, of course, be some situations that call for special handling, but the majority can be taken care of by these so-called form letters. The "special" letters should be carefully written, typed, gone over, improved, and retyped before being sent out. They should *not* be hastily dictated along with the rest of the mail. I repeat, collection letters are important and deserving of all the time necessary to make them effective. Please notice that I used the phrase "so-called form letters." They should be "form" letters only insofar as the same "form" is being sent to a number of people. Don't let them be "form" letters in the sense that they *read* like "form" letters.

A collection letter, or indeed any other kind of letter can *appear* personal whether it is or not. The minute your customer sees what he believes to be a "form" letter, he says, "Just a routine letter. We can hold them up a while longer." On the other hand, if he receives a typewritten letter that reads as if you were looking right at him instead of at a large group of delinquent accounts, he may sit up and take notice.

Here are a few tips about the writing and sending out of collection letters:

Be prompt—send some statement of the amount, either with the merchandise or shortly after.

Be regular—no customer objects to being reminded of his obligation, providing the reminder is regular and courteous.

Don't apologize for asking for money after it is due. You only make it easier for him to disregard your request.

Don't be too lenient—unless you don't need the money and don't ever expect to.

Don't let anger, contempt, or pity get into any of your letters—these are emotions that practically never lead to the payment of bills.

Be a little firmer in your demand with each follow-up—

write courteously, frankly, but let him know you mean business.

Show fairness all the time—and in the early letters give the man every opportunity to tell you if your bill is wrong. Sometimes bills are wrong, and then complications of a serious nature are likely to develop.

Let us assume that you have subdivided your delinquent accounts into the three groups as suggested:

Group 1: good customers—good pay
Group 2: good customers—slow pay
Group 3: questionable customers—poor pay

Now we'll take three concrete examples, all built around the same situation.

Smith Brothers and Jones owe you $263.50 for merchandise delivered and accepted forty-five days ago. You sent a bill with or shortly after the goods were shipped, just to make sure their understanding agreed with yours as to the amount. In thirty days you sent along the usual statement. Two weeks later we'll say you wrote a simple reminder letter, something like this:

This is just a little friendly reminder—that our bill to you of January 6th for $263.50 is still unpaid.

If there is any question about the amount, won't you please tell us so that the matter can be straightened out? And if it's just a case of being overlooked, won't you please put a check in the return mail?

Thanks very much.

That letter may or may not apply to your business. If it does —and you want to—please feel free to go ahead and use it.

Another two weeks go by, and you receive neither word nor money. Here is a suggestion for handling Group 1 (good customer—good pay).

You have been so very prompt in your payments in the past that we can't understand what has happened to our January 6th bill for $263.50.

Are we at fault in some way—has the bill just been mislaid—or is there some adjustment pending that we aren't familiar with? Won't you be kind enough to either send us a check (if our bill is correct) or write and tell us just exactly what the situation is?

Here's the way Group 2 (good customer—slow pay) might be approached:

Probably the most difficult letter that we have to write is the letter to a good customer who doesn't pay his bills as promptly as we like them paid.

We appreciate his business—we don't like to annoy him—and yet our terms of 2% 10 days, 30 days net must be lived up to, or our own obligations can't be met.

You'll see the fairness in that, I'm sure. Our bill of January 6th for $263.50 is over two months old now and thirty days overdue. Won't you please send us your check by return mail—so that you'll be all straight on our books again? You'll feel better about it and so will we.

And here's a letter that might be used to Group 3 (questionable customer—poor pay):

When a bill becomes 2 months old, it's time to do something about it, isn't it?

On January 6th, we billed you for $263.50—subject to our regular terms of 2% 10 days net—for merchandise delivered to you late in December.

Two weeks after the bill should have been paid, we asked whether there was any question as to the amount. Nothing happened.

Now we are always glad to accommodate our customers

but you realize, don't you, that there must be a limit? We can't go on being lenient forever and expect to stay in business. You don't want us to take legal steps to collect this bill and neither do we. Won't you therefore put a check in the return mail—so that your credit standing with us will be as it should be?

Thank you.

Remember that every collection letter should aim to collect the money, but at no sacrifice of good will. Try to maintain an even balance between the two objectives. Don't work so hard for the money that the customer will be "off you forever." And don't be so friendly and lenient that the customer reads between the lines and decides that you really aren't in earnest about it.

Let every recipient of one of your collection letters think your letter is addressed to him and him only. Use form letters if you will, but make them personal—*and human.*

Here are a number of collection letters that were successful because they *were human,* yet *right to the point.*

Dear Dr. ———:

HOW GOOD IS YOUR MEMORY?

Ours would be admittedly bad if we did not keep audited records. These records show you still owe us $28.50.

Remember now?

Thanks in advance for your check.

Dear Mr. ———:

How often have we heard it said, "I should write a letter tonight but I can't seem to get started!"

You don't have to write us a letter. It's so much easier to write a check. Your unpaid account is $41.

Thank you!

Dear Dr. ———:

A baby on your doorstep!

That may sound like a startling statement and the chances are it may never literally happen to you. But it does happen to us.

What I'm trying to say is this. The "baby" in this case is your unpaid account of $114. It's been on our "doorstep" a long time past maturity date.

Your check will enable me to find it a happy home, the bank, to join its brother and sister checks.

Thank you!

Dear Mr. ———:

His wife was working . . .

a crossword puzzle. She turned to him and asked: "Darling, what is a three-letter word that means a female sheep?"

He replied: "Ewe, dearest!" and another family fight was on.

The five-letter word we are interested in is the other one for money . . . "Check." Please send us one for $65, before you again forget to do so and thanks in advance.

Dear Mr. ———:

You've probably heard . . .

this little story of the young country couple who were getting married.

After the wedding, the happy bridegroom said to the parson, "Shall I pay your usual fee now? Or shall I wait a year and send you $100.00?"

Without any hesitation the preacher replied, "I'll take the $3.00 now."

Why wait until you can send all of your unpaid balance of $84? Send a convenient payment now. We'll appreciate it and we won't mind waiting a little longer for the balance.

Fair enuff?

Point No. 14. Put the Apostrophe to Good Use

This pointer is about *contractions,* and personally, I am heartily in favor of them—in their proper place. Many people aren't, and I agree that there are times when the use of contractions is unnecessary and even improper. There are *more* times, however, when intelligent use of a contraction injects into the letter that spontaneity and naturalness so necessary to the *friendly feeling* we are striving for.

A really *good* letter, when read aloud, won't sound like a letter at all. If it is naturally written, you will subconsciously visualize the writer delivering that same message in person. You will subconsciously concentrate on the message itself rather than on the way it is expressed.

If that then is our goal—and in my opinion it certainly is—then anything we can do in our letters to make them less letterish and more natural will be a step in the right direction.

How many people go through even one day without using at least some contractions in speaking? Not many—and that's easily verified. On all sides, in every office, on every corner, and in every home you hear:

> "Hot, isn't it?"
> "How's business?"
> "Here's a chance to make money."
> "That's our trouble, too."
> "What's the matter?"
> "Aren't you through yet?"
> "Doesn't this look great?"

How artificial and affected we'd sound if we talked like this:

"Hot, is it not?"
"Do you not know better?"
"Are you not getting stouter?"
"Does not this look nice?"

Sometimes, letters which don't take advantage of the naturalness of contractions are likewise artificial and affected. Instead of reading smoothly and evenly, you get a series of breaks that emphasize the fact that this is just a cold-blooded, formal message on paper, not a warm, friendly substitution for a personal talk.

Here's an excerpt from a letter that makes good use of contractions:

If you'll send us your renewal instructions *now*, we'll credit the $3 already paid against the yearly fee of $18, leaving you only $15 to pay to extend your subscription for a FULL YEAR from the end of your trial. This will give you your 13-week trial subscription FREE—you'll receive a total of 15 months' service, instead of 12, for the regular fee of $18.

Let's talk now about the borderline cases—the instances where it doesn't sound stilted or unnatural not to use the contraction but where using it strengthens the message.

I should rather start off a letter with *"Here's an opportunity to save money"* than with *"Here is an opportunity to save money."* That's a borderline example, of course. It is a strong sentence either way, but it is a little stronger, I feel, with the contraction.

In the last analysis, letters are judged not so much by the quality of their grammatical construction as by *the extent to which they make a favorable impression.*

Assignment. *Look over some of your letters from the stand-point of contractions. Do you use them now? If not, should you? Do some experimenting.*

Point No. 15. Don't Make Your Letters TELEGRAMS

This is about telegraphic writing, which means taking the wrong kind of short cut. It is so named because it resembles the composition of telegrams, where words cost money. The words to leave out of a letter are the meaningless and *unnecessary* words that serve only to make the letter longer—not the little connecting words like "the," "if," "we," "us," "that," and "a," which when omitted make the letter jumpy and telegraphic.

Don't misunderstand. We are striving, always, for conciseness. We want the letter as short as we can make it and still have it tell a complete, friendly story—but there's a limit. If you've been writing "Enclosed please find a folder," you can cut out a word by saying "Enclosed is a folder." But if the sentence is "We are glad to report that your books were mailed Tuesday," you can't cut out the word "your" and make the statement read "We are glad to report that books were mailed Tuesday." You can, of course, but not without making your letter telegraphic and therefore unnatural.

Bear in mind that your aim is to write natural, friendly letters which *sound* natural and friendly when they are read.

Being telegraphic is just a habit—but one that will hamper your efforts to write interesting letters. Here are some examples taken from actual correspondence which illustrate the point. The word in parentheses is the one which had been left out.

Note. We are talking now only about being telegraphic, so no mention will be made of stereotyped phrases or other shortcomings in the following sentences:

(We) acknowledge herewith your reply to our letter

(Your) order will be filled in accordance with your instructions

(We) regret very much to find

Under the circumstances, (we) would suggest

Upon receipt of your reply, (we) will have our mail division

Kindly check over (the) above figures

Cutting down the cost of correspondence is important, but it is false economy to eliminate words when doing so decreases the effectiveness or humanness of the letter.

Look on every letter as a flesh-and-blood representative of your company. Every letter you send out makes some kind of impression. If your letters are telegraphic, the people reading them can't help but feel either that you don't care enough about them to write a decent letter or that you haven't the time to give them the attention they deserve.

On the other hand, if you write naturally, interestingly, and at the same time concisely, you have done a good public relations job in addition to the original function of the letter.

How you say it is every bit as important as what you say. Therefore, write letters—*not telegrams.*

Point No. 16. Make the APPEARANCE of Your Letters an Asset

There is a distinct advantage in personal contact that is not enjoyed by letters.

The modulation of the voice, the interpretive glance of the eye, the contraction and relaxation of the muscles, the posture of the body, the opportunity for "rebuttal"—all these things emphasize the spoken message. For this reason, a personal interview is nearly always the most effective method of handling any kind of transaction.

It would be nice if every inquiry could be answered personally, if all complaints could be diplomatically smoothed out in personal session, perhaps at luncheon, with the complainant.

The impracticability of all this calls, of course, for correspondence. The inquiry, the complaint, the adjustment—all must be handled via the mails.

Come back now to where we started—the advantage a personal visit has over a mail visit. The thing to do is to find for correspondence some way to make up, at least partially, the deficiency, so that the contents or message in your letter will get an even break.

What—in a letter—corresponds to the appearance of the individual? *The physical appearance of the envelope and letterhead, the character of the paper, the quality of the typewriting and the setup of the letter on the page.*

What impression do *your* letters make on the people who receive them *before* they read them?

Look on the *appearance* of your letters as you would on the appearance of a salesman. Make it impressive and inviting. Insist on uniformly good typewriting, exercising care as to the salutation, margins, paragraphs, spacing, close, etc.

A Good Salesman Looks the Part

—and since a good letter *is* a good salesman, it, too, should look the part. The neat, attractive appearance of a salesman doesn't actually close any sales, but it sure helps a lot. Likewise the appearance of your letters can help *them* get off to a good start, can provide a helpful assist for the job they have to do.

The next time you receive letters from your secretary for signing, look at them *critically*. Consider the impression they make before you start to read. Are they clean-looking, invit-

ing? Any untidy erasures? Are they neatly set up on the page
—neither top- nor bottom-heavy, nor lopsided?

The first paragraph should be short, interesting, friendly,
easy to read. *None* of the paragraphs should be much over
an inch or so in depth, otherwise they become *difficult* to
read. Use either the block or indented style, whichever you
prefer, but see that the net result is pleasing to the eye. *Appearance is important.*

Assignment. *Make an appraisal of your firm's stationery.
Try to visualize what kind of impression it would make on
you if you knew nothing about the company. Now judge
the appearance of your typewritten letters before they go out.
Are they an asset or a liability?*

Point No. 17. Cut the Cloth to Fit the Pattern

Here is the answer to *How long should a letter be? The*
question comes up frequently and there are two answers.

Generally speaking, *a letter should be as long as necessary
to tell the story effectively—no longer and no shorter.* Give
the message in a clear-cut, straightforward manner, garnish it
with a friendly entrance and exit, and let that be all.

Specifically speaking, however, some letters should be long
and others short, depending upon their *purpose.*

If the object is to answer an inquiry, the proper telling of
the story will, in many cases, necessitate a long letter. Usually
a person who asks for information will read nearly anything
you send him on the subject, for he has already expressed interest. A short letter, hastily skipping over the points that
might well be elaborated, goes about halfway and is seldom
effective.

If the object is to solicit an inquiry, tell only enough to
make the prospect want to hear more. In some cases, that
might mean one short paragraph.

And it might be that three or four paragraphs, or even two pages, would be necessary in order to create enough interest to make the prospect want to hear more. *Don't shoot your ammunition at once.* Tell enough—but not too much.

If the object is to collect money, the tendency should be toward comparatively short letters—three or four paragraphs at the most.

If the object is to adjust a complaint, don't go out of your way to write a short letter. Explain the situation fully. Don't let people think that you get so many complaints that you can't take time to answer them courteously and completely. That merely fans the flame.

Be guided by what the letter is supposed to do. Think about it first and then act accordingly.

Here is a letter that is as long as it should be, and yet it consists of only one paragraph.

Gentlemen:

We have just perfected a new type billing machine that will reduce your accounting costs by fully FIFTY PER CENT. To whom in your organization should we send full details?

Sincerely,

And here is a letter that covered four full pages, yet wasn't too long considering the character of its message and the fact that it was sent to former guests.

Dear Friend of Ours and of Capon Springs:

"May 1st is a long way off, but the lovely memories of that beautiful and peaceful spot in the mountains of West Virginia keep our spirits going. Look for us on opening day."

You may not be among those who have written us dur-

ing the winter months, but haven't you, too, felt it coming over you—that dreamy, almost irresistible urge to be
amidst the beauty, peacefulness and sheer joy of living
which Nature has made so much a part of Capon Springs?

The fast pace of modern life, the pressure under which
most of us work and live, make so great the need for a
haven where the spirit can be free, where the mind can
dwell in quiet meditation, and where the body might
be refreshed and energy renewed for the days ahead.

Your greetings and letters reaching us around Christmas time told us of memories that live with you throughout the year. Memories that give a lift and a glow even in
the midst of winter's cold and snow. Memories of little
things, little in themselves but somehow doing things to
the heart. Memories that transport you far from the tur-
moil of the city to a secluded valley where people just
naturally fall into being their true selves and fall out of
what our present overcivilization is tending to make
them.

Memories of a spot off the beaten path where nourish-
ment is given to both body and spirit; the body fed by
ample, wholesome, home-grown, home-cooked food; by
clean, bracing mountain air and by relaxing, restful
sleep; the spirit nourished by countless manifestations of
friendship and good will, in which your part is both
recipient and contributor. Only memories these, hazy
memories, but at surprising turns, they flood the mind
and soul, bringing sometimes a smile, perhaps a chuckle,
but always a glow.

How important are these "little" things to a real vacation! Too often are they denied the one most needing
them. Said a noted medical authority on relaxation:

"Stimulation must not be confused with relaxation, as it has been for so long. I dread the days when my blood pressure patients return from their vacations."

You know, from your experience at Capon, a vacation can yield both fun and relaxation. The fun you have here is of the natural, spontaneous type, requiring no stimulation. And as for relaxation, you know this is no part-way thing at Capon. It's an "all-out" feature. No formality, no dressing up. Men do not wear coats or ties in the dining room. Taking a coat and tie off a man sorta strips him of the veneer of city life and gives him a chance to be his natural self. We realize that not all men like this. (Nor do all wives.) But then these folks don't come to Capon.

You, who do spend your vacations here, come knowing the kind of place Capon is, knowing its limitations, knowing too that you can depend on that completely at-home feeling and on being among other kind and sincere folks, who have never a thought of trying to impress you by their dress, position, or wealth. Friendships you have formed here have remained and grown with the years and are rekindled by repeated meetings at Capon year after year.

To preserve and protect this friendly atmosphere, we shall continue our policy of no advertising and of accepting reservations only from old friends and their friends. "Like coming home"—your greeting to us on arriving— is the way we always want Capon to be for you.

While we plan nothing that will change the atmosphere of friendliness and simplicity you have helped create here, it does not mean we will stand still so far as material comforts are concerned. Indeed not. You will find, this year, much in the way of increased conveniences and pleasures. You have already expressed your delight at the wonderful night's rest enjoyed on the airfoam super-cushioned mattress toppers we introduced last year.

This season, we are getting around to insuring enough heat in every room to take care of any sudden cold or damp spell. Now you'll be able to have heat whenever you want it in your room. This will appeal particularly to those who like Capon best in the Spring or Fall. And, of course, the huge fireplaces make the living rooms and dining rooms colorful as well as comfortable. It is not necessary to say anything about the rooms being cool during the summer. As you know, blankets at Capon are a must, through almost the whole season.

Other things and improvements? Rooms are brighter, shower baths better, hot water facilities improved; golf course better than ever, in addition to an improved pitch course, a practice putting green and a driving range to practice on; more turf bowling, better shuffleboards; weekly lunches on the lawn, moonlight dances, etc. There will be increased trained supervision for young children so that their parents can feel freer.

No really big things, but as we well know, you don't want "big" things at Capon. What we are adding is in the way of greater comfort and more fun, nothing "ritzy" or "putting on the dog." Things you would do if you were doing the job for us. The old wooden bathhouses at the pool are gone, affording a greatly improved natural set-ting and at the same time allowing considerably more space for sunbathers.

Tucked away almost out of sight is a brand new "HONEYMOON COTTAGE" reserved for newlyweds. If you have friends who are planning their honeymoon between April 30th and November 1st, have them phone or write for reservations promptly. Our wedding gift to all honey-mooners will be a special rate plus a gift package of Capon food products to start them off in housekeeping.

Here's news that may be of interest to young ladies not yet honeymoon bound, but hoping. There should be more young men at Capon this season! Ready this Spring will be a young men's dormitory situated at our Iron Spring Farm around the bend from Capon. Here from eight to ten young men can have all the things everyone else gets at Capon at a considerably reduced cost.

The old Capon standbys will, of course, be on hand. Our deep freeze plant is well stocked with meats of various kinds, including our home-grown turkeys, ducks, chickens, lamb, etc. Roasts and steaks, served more often last year than ever, will be found quite regularly on the menu, and the steak dinner broiled outdoors on the hill is one of those things your letters tell us lingers in your memory. Our breeding of pure-bred hogs purchased from the Government Farms at Beltsville, Md., has resulted in greatly improved meat. You will find Capon bacons and hams the best we have ever served, both having a minimum of fat and plenty of delicious lean meat.

The fresh vegetables and fruits raised on our farms will be even more varied, and many of them, fresh frozen, are waiting the early comers. On the table as always will be Pearl's apple butter, honey from our own and neighboring beehives, milk, cream, and butter, products of our own cows, and eggs from hens at our farm, five minutes from the dining table.

As for rates for next season, you may have already heard about our policy in this regard. We announced it last Christmas to all purchasers of Capon Springs turkeys. At a time when the price of turkeys had risen 10¢ a pound between Thanksgiving and Christmas, we adhered to the lower price, stating that "prices were already too high." In that letter last Christmas we added:

"If enough of us act, we may be able to stop the spiral of inflation before it stops us. We feel rather strongly about this, and are promising you now, regardless of costs and what others may do, rates at Capon will *not* be increased over last year. Wherever possible, we will lower them. Nor will this be done by sacrificing the improvements planned or at the expense of our co-workers, who will receive a pay increase, a policy we have followed for virtually all of our 16 years. We are going right ahead with our plans."

We now state definitely that rates for this season covering each and every guest will be *lower* than last year. And for parties of three or more couples in either May or October, the reductions will amount to 12½%.

The celebrations of Christmas on June 25th (the halfway mark) and on September 25th (the ¾ mark) have been so well received by you that they have been incorporated as fixtures into Capon living. After all, it's the *spirit* of Christmas that really counts. That wonderful spirit should not be limited to once a year. All of us agree that if the spirit of Christmas could be spread around the calendar, many, if not all, of mankind's problems would be solved.

We cannot close without a note of thanks, deep, sincere, and heartfelt. We of the Austin family are grateful for your friendship and love and for all that you have done for this little but blessed valley. Capon owes more to you than you realize. You "have builded better than you know," even to making last season better than the one before, a better season despite the fact that out of increased receipts came greatly reduced earnings. Better because our ties with old friends were made closer plus the added pleasure of making new friends.

We look forward to your coming, get real happiness out of your being here, and feel regret at your departing. You have by your kindness and affection elevated us from just innkeepers to friends with whom you are enjoying a stay. All nine of us will be on hand to greet you when you come.

THE AUSTINS of CAPON SPRINGS

Point No. 18. Make Your Letters SMOOTH

Did you ever hear of *suction* in letter writing?

Suction is that quality in a letter which literally "drags" the reader from one paragraph to the next until he has read the letter through. The Capon Springs letter you have just read is an excellent example.

Other words for "suction" are *continuity, smoothness,* an easy flow of connected thoughts that carry the reader logically from the first paragraph to the second, from the second to the third, from the third to the fourth, and so on. Notice the suction in this letter:

"For goodness' sake! Get me a blotter that BLOTS!"

We heard a business executive growl this at his secretary one day while he was signing some checks. And you can easily understand his annoyance. A *good* blotter builds good will—a sleazy, inefficient blotter inspires nothing but *"cuss"* words.

That's why we like to sell WRENN BLOTTING. This is the thirsty long-lasting stock that writers *like* to keep around.

Highly absorbent over a long period of time, WRENN BLOTTING has the quality appearance that lends itself to endless attractive printing designs.

You'll like WRENN BLOTTING, too. Not just because it means a lot of customer satisfaction—but because it's an *easy* stock to print. Reduces press time because it doesn't fuzz or shed lint. Takes ink beautifully, too.

Call us when you need a really superior grade of blotter stock. And remember that WRENN BLOTTING is only one of hundreds of nationally known papers from leading mills available at Garrett-Buchanan.

Point No. 19. For Secretaries Only

If, along with your boss, you've read the pages which preceded this one, you know, of course, what we are trying to accomplish. Perhaps you have already noticed a change in the character of the messages you have been typing—a tendency toward friendlier, warmer, more natural-sounding letters.

During the transition, you have probably watched, I hope with interest and satisfaction, a gradual reduction in the use of old-fashioned, meaningless words and phrases, less tendency to ramble and beat around the bush, more genuine interest in the other fellow than in "we, our, and us." That's *good*—exactly what the doctor ordered.

But the job of writing really good letters is a big one—too big a responsibility for one person. If you're the good secretary I think you are, you won't make your boss carry the entire load. You'll make an important contribution yourself. And it will be more—*much, much more* than just accurate transcribing and good, clean typing.

Generally speaking, you're the "Vice-President" in charge of the physical appearance of your boss's letters, the *"first impression"* they create as the result of attractive positioning on the page. If they are *inviting* to look at, they help get the message off to a good start, and that means a lot.

But there's so much more you can do to make yourself a valuable assistant.

In her excellent "STANDARD HANDBOOK FOR SECRETARIES," Lois Hutchinson gives some very useful pointers under the heading "Efficient Method of Preparing Letters." (Incidentally, if you don't have this book on your desk, handy at all times, you're missing a good bet. It is one of the best books on the subject I have ever seen. Published by McGraw-Hill.)

Proofread each letter as it is finished. If this is done, all typed letters will be ready at any time they might be called for. Do not write several letters and then proofread them.

Proofread slowly so that no typographical errors will be overlooked. No defense can be offered for these. Check carefully all initials, addresses, reference numbers, and the spelling of words not frequently used.

Every page must be immaculately clean: no struck-over letters, no half erasures, and no finger marks or smudges.

Clip the pages of each letter together in the upper left corner, not in the center, nor on the right.

Clip pencil notations to letters that require special handling. These notations can remind the dictator of things to be done, as "Check to accompany this," "Date necessary," "Enclosures necessary," "To be held," etc.

If there is a question about a certain letter, write it on a note and clip it to the letter; the dictator can then answer when he returns the letter and at his convenience.

In special instances when another than the dictator is

to sign the letter, clip a note to that effect over the place for signature. This will prevent the dictator from absent-mindedly signing the letter.

When handing in letters, put them in a manila file folder on which is marked "For Signature." The manila folder not only keeps the letters all together so that they can be considered at one time, but keeps them clean, and keeps them private.

Arrange the letters in the folder in the order of their importance; the most important always on top.

It is not necessary to clip the envelopes or enclosures to the letters (unless the dictator prefers that this is done). This extra bulk makes the letters awkward to handle when they are being signed.

Address the envelopes from the carbon copies, while the letters are being read and signed. *This saves time.* Assume responsibility for correct addresses, the manner of dispatch of letters, and enclosures. If any change is made in an address on a signed letter, correct the envelope first, then the letter.

* * *

ENGLISH—As She Is Wrote

Far be it from me to delve very deeply into the subject of English Grammar, for there are too many of you who know more about it than I do. The fact is, I agree heartily with Author John O'London when he said—

My point of view is that, in everyday life, good English follows clear thinking rather than that system of rules called Grammar which youth loathes and maturity forgets.

But there are a number of misconceptions (or perhaps just question marks) that I should like to clear up, again using that highly respected authority Lois Hutchinson as a backstop.

Sentences do not necessarily have to have a subject or verb. A phrase *may* stand as a sentence—*and often does.*

A sentence *may* end with a preposition. Sometimes the final preposition is superfluous or awkward, but more often it is a very effective ending.

A sentence *may* correctly begin with "and," "but," "for," "or," etc. It is usually started thus for emphasis, or as a continuation or a summing up.

Singulars and plurals *may* be logically used in the same sentence. However, the best practice is to make all singulars conform to singulars and all plurals to plurals, where nothing is to be gained by writing them otherwise.

Although there is much prejudice against the split infinitive, *it has been used by good writers of all times.* In many cases, a split infinitive is to be preferred to any arrangement that suggests stiffness, or permits vagueness or ambiguity.

Dagger and Double Dagger

Yes, and Dieresis, Circumflex, Cedilla, Tilde, Caret, Ellipsis—do you know what they are? They are included in the more than thirty different Marks of Punctuation that are available to you when you type a letter. But don't let them confuse you. In most cases, you'll only have occasion to use the everyday variety, like the comma, semicolon, colon, period, question mark, exclamation mark, etc.

There are forty-seven meaty pages on the subject in the Standard Handbook, so obviously we can't even hit the high spots.

But I do want to make this one point—

Punctuation is a matter of judgment, not of definite rule. It should be used to add expression and meaning to written words. Like pepper and salt, however, it should be used *sparingly*. Too much is just as bad as none at all.

How to Make a Hit with Your Boss

Be on time in the morning. Nothing signifies an interest in the work more than being on time in the morning and at noon, and not *"watching the clock"* to get away in the evening.

Make very few personal appointments that will consume office time.

Learn to work with a system. Improve as many conditions as can be improved, and have as many things as possible working mechanically each day, or performed as a habit under a well-thought-out system.

Attempt to see always from the other's viewpoint. Try once in a while to face the problems an employer is facing in his endeavor to make ends meet. If he seems annoyed at times, there might be a chance that he has a right to be.

Listen attentively—not nervously—to all instructions that are given, and act understandingly.

Make a list of things to do on dull days, and do them. Here are a few suggestions: Rearrange parts of filing system; clean supply cabinet and check for restocking; clean desk and restock with supplies; clean up office generally, making it neater by clearing away any papers or other articles that have a tendency to accumulate uselessly; inaugurate newer and more efficient methods where needed; have repairs made to anything in need of them; do cataloguing, listing, or filing to improve later work or perfect office routine; practice shorthand; address envelopes for routine work.

Assignment. *Have a friendly talk with your stenographer and start the wheels toward some effective teamwork.*

Point No. 20. Check Up on Yourself Too

Let's now put the shoe on the other foot. *What do you think* YOUR *attributes should be?* Suppose we list the qualities, of a good correspondent and see how they look:

> Initiative
> Good judgment
> Resourcefulness
> Capacity for mental development
> Willingness to improve
> Amenability to correction
> Cooperative spirit
> Good manners
> Knowledge of English composition and good diction
> Knowledge of sources of information
> Knowledge of other divisions and departments
> Ability to give clear and explicit instructions
> Ability to concentrate and complete work in the shortest possible time
> Ability to grasp the elements of a letter quickly
> Ability to think in terms of the "other fellow"

Assignment. *Read them again and see how* YOU *measure up.*

Point No. 21. Develop a Good Form-letter System

There are many times when one letter applies equally well to a number of cases, and if that happens in your office, the need for some system of *form* letters is apparent.

There are certain routine situations—such as answering some kinds of inquiries, adjusting some kinds of complaints—in which "form" letters will answer the purpose just as well and in many cases more effectively than dictated letters. If there are enough instances like that, you should install a form-letter system.

Note. A form letter should never be used unless it *completely* covers the particular situation. If it doesn't seem to "fit," even in the slightest detail, then an individually written letter, possibly using the form letter as a model, would be infinitely better. It is false economy to *make* a letter fit when it actually doesn't.

Let's get straight on the real meaning of the word "form" as used in connection with letters. This discussion has nothing to do with the so-called form *sales* letters but applies only to routine correspondence. A form letter is simply any letter, either dictated hastily or painstakingly prepared, that is sent to a number of people instead of just one individual. The right kind of form letter will not *look* like a form letter at all. It will be individually typed and hand signed and will have exactly the appearance of a personally dictated letter.

The effectiveness of a form letter is killed if the letter *looks* "*form-letterish.*" The way to avoid that is to write out in longhand a friendly, convincing, interesting, and complete letter to cover the particular need you have in mind. Then have it typewritten. Go over it again; analyze it to see if it meets the requirements; blue-pencil it; work on it until you feel that *as a personal letter* it "fills the bill." Then use it as a "form" letter every time it fits.

If the letter is going to a number of people instead of to only one, there is even more reason why it should be good. If we are interested in impressions, then surely the use of a form letter would give us an opportunity to get a multiple reaction or impression, multiplying by many times the *favorable* impression we could make with any one letter.

Remember, however, that "form" letters can be a factor for evil as well as for good. They will hamper our efforts to build good will if they give the impression that we are standoffish or uninterested.

First thing to do, of course, is to list the situations that can be handled just as well by a made-up letter as by a personally dictated one. Then write letters to fit each case. Most people can write in longhand or typewrite better letters than they can dictate, but you do whichever seems easiest and best for you.

When you've turned out what you believe are good letters and appropriate for their purpose, put them aside for a while. Look at them next morning with a fresh, unbiased (if possible) viewpoint. Read them aloud. Do they *look* and *sound* like *personally dictated* letters? They *should*.

Do they completely cover the situations for which they are intended? (*Don't ever use a form letter unless it exactly fits the circumstances.*)

Do they sound *friendly, sincere?*

Would they make a good impression on *you* if you were on the receiving end?

In setting up a practical form-letter system, which you can only do after a careful analysis of recent and typical letter carbons, the secret lies in having just the right number of letters. Too *few*—and you aren't saving as much dictating time as you might. Too *many*—and the system becomes unwieldy. It takes too long to find the appropriate letter and if that happens very often you'll get discouraged and stop using the system altogether.

Point No. 22. About Letter Qualities You Can SEE

Points No. 22 and No. 23 are *"yardsticks"* to measure the effectiveness of your letters *after* you have written them. This one has to do with the visible qualities, the things you can *"put your hands on."* You can look at the letter after it's typed and immediately pick out the physical shortcomings, if any exist, and correct them.

I don't just mean physical appearance, although that is, of

course, important. It is obvious that your letters should be neatly typed and invitingly set up on the page. The margins should be even and sufficiently large to avoid that crowded look. Spelling and punctuation should be correct in every detail. All in all, the letter should be as interesting-looking as you can make it.

But you can *see* more in a letter than just physical appearance.

Have you stopped using all stereotyped and worn-out words and phrases?

Does the opening sentence do more than just acknowledge?

Is your letter sharp and concise and to the point—or rambling and wordy?

Is your answer complete?

Does it cover the subject fully?—or only partially?

Are the various thoughts and paragraphs related and does the letter read smoothly—or do you flit around from one point to another and hope the message will be understood?

Are there any great long sentences that require a new breath in the middle?

Are the paragraphs short and easy to read?

Is your letter free from vague terms and big words?

Letter writing is somewhat like golf—there are a lot of things to remember. The advantage that we have in letter writing, however, is that we can without penalty go over our work *after* it's done—analyze it, actually see it, and size it up.

Get into the habit of mentally tearing your letters to pieces. Do that, and no matter how good the letters you write now, you'll soon see a very tangible improvement.

Point No. 23. About Letter Qualities You Just FEEL

The second *yardstick* is for the things in a letter that you *feel* rather than see. This is the psychological part.

You read a letter and somehow get a negative reaction. There's nothing about the letter you can honestly object to and nothing at all that you can lay your hands on—still there's *something* that didn't quite "set" the right way.

You read another letter, and for some reason you warm up from the start. That letter has the right tone—it is written with the deliberate idea of making friends.

It is pretty generally conceded that a salesman—before he can sell a product—*must sell himself*. He either is liked and creates confidence in himself and therefore sells—or he doesn't. If he doesn't sell, it often is because he hasn't made friends.

Letters are that way, too. Regular, routine, everyday letters that aren't sent out to sell at all can, by their very tone, affect the public feeling toward the company sending them out.

In what way will your letter change your reader's regard for your firm? That's the thing to consider. Will it make him more friendly or less friendly, or will the status remain the same?

You don't want to stop at just having your letter do its job. *Make it do more than that!* Make *every* letter a *sales* letter regardless of its purpose.

To Sum Up, Write unto Others

The Golden Rule applies to letter writing just as much as to any other function of business.

The trouble with most of us is that we think the job is completed when we're through dictating. Fact is, the *writing* of a letter doesn't mean a thing *until the letter has reached its destination, has been read and understood, has created a favorable impression of you and your company*. Write, therefore, with the *reader* in mind. Write as you would like to be written *to*.

$\mathbf{A}$re the recipients of a form letter applying for a job under any obligation to acknowledge it, whether they are interested or not? Of course not, if it is obviously a form letter (however personal in appearance), any more than they are obligated to answer the hundred and one circulars that come to them every day. But while you don't have to as a matter of business courtesy, sending a friendly acknowledgment and perhaps a word of encouragement is a *nice* thing to do. And good public relations. The following such answer is a lot better than no answer, but it would have done the sender even more good if it had been less stereotyped.

Thank you for favoring us with card of application for employment.

While your background and experience are interesting, we regret to advise that at the present time there are no vacancies nor opportunities to consider the employment of additional personnel in our agency.

We shall maintain an active interest in your application, however, and should an opportunity present itself in the future, we shall be pleased to advise you.

In your letters, I hope you're staying away from such expressions as *"favoring"*—*"we regret to advise"*—*"we shall be pleased"*—etc.

Okay to Say "The Writer"?

Definitely *not*. The objective in all letter writing is to create a good substitute for a *personally* delivered message. The more *impersonal* your letter, the less chance it has of making a favorable impression. I am indebted to one of my readers for sending in the following gem, a fine illustration of the misuse of the word *"writer."*

> In connection with your letter of November 1 to the *writer,* it is impossible for the *writer* ever to predetermine exactly when he will be in town and for that reason it is suggested that should you be in Baltimore and want to pay a visit at our office you call the *writer* prior to your coming here.

Note—the writer must have had his mind on the *writer*.

While we're picking on it, notice that this letter commits another crime. It's all one sentence, and too long for what it says. Let's rewrite it and see if we can't eliminate the weaknesses.

> Thank you for your letter of November 1.
>
> Unfortunately, I am never quite sure when I'll be in town so it isn't easy to make appointments.
>
> The next time you are in Baltimore, if you'd like to pay us a visit, give me a call first and I'll certainly try and arrange to see you.

Isn't that better, and a lot *friendlier?*

"If There's Anything I Hate—"

This section is dedicated to the highlighting of some of the *little* things we do in correspondence that cause annoyance. Granted, we do them unconsciously (if at all) but that doesn't make them any less irritating.

The case of the illegible signature

What a *pain* it is to try and decipher a signature that looks like a cross between a chicken scratch and some hieroglyphics. Don't take any chances with *yours*. If there's any doubt about it, always have your name typed below the pen signature. Don't make people *guess*.

The case of Mrs. versus Miss

Every once in a while we get a letter signed by one of the fair sex that leaves us up in the air completely as to how to address her. As for instance—Mary B. Smith. We don't know her well enough to say "Dear Mary" or even "Dear Mary Smith." So we're forced to the formal salutation—name of company, address, *"attention, Mary B. Smith,* Gentlemen:".

There's nothing wrong with that, of course, but you can write a friendlier letter if you are in a position to start it out "Dear Mrs. Smith" or "Dear Miss Smith." So if you're a gal with some letters to sign, please don't keep us in the dark. Below your signature, type your name with *Miss* or *Mrs.* in parentheses right before it. (Mrs.) Mary B. Smith. Then we'll *know*.

And please don't make us guess your sex either, as we must when you sign M. B. Smith. If your name is Mary, you won't like to be addressed "Dear Mr. Smith," but that is the way it will be if you don't make it clear.

The case of the rubber stamp

Not too often, but every once in a while, we see a letter with a *rubber stamp signature*. Usually it is on a circular letter of some kind, but even so there's no excuse for it. If a personal signature isn't practical, use a good facsimile made with a signature cut and run with the rest of the letter. You may not fool anybody but at least the letter will make a much better impression.

The case of the absent dictator

In this situation, our "hero" dictates a flock of letters in the morning, then tells his secretary that he has an important date in the afternoon (FORE!) and won't be back. The letters go out with this notation at the bottom: *"Dictated, but not read."* It's almost like saying *"Written, but without interest."*

If you find you're not going to be around to sign letters, our suggestion is to do one of two things—(a) have them held until you *can* sign them, or (b) have an associate read and sign your name to them. (If there is anything of a legal or official nature in the letters, the signer should put his own initials under the signature.)

Here's another minor crime in letter writing which invariably gets the message off on the wrong foot. This one is the result of plain carelessness and there's really no excuse for it.

The case of the misspelled name

Of course, you wouldn't let this happen in *your* office, but all too frequently we see letters with glaring mistakes right in the salutation. The worst we've ever seen was in a letter we received recently—

> Mr. Earle A. Buckley
> The Bickley Institute
> Lincoln-Liberty Bldg.
> Dear Mr. Backley:

Index